✳ THEOLOGICAL TIMES ✳

THEOLOGICAL TIMES

AN AUTOBIOGRAPHICAL REVIEW

James Farris

Mosa Press
Victoria, British Columbia

© 2015 W. J. S. Farris

All rights reserved. No part of this publication may be reproduced, stored, or transmitted in any form or by any means without the written permission of the publisher or a photocopying licence from Access Copyright, Toronto, Canada.

Scripture quotations are from *New Revised Standard Version Bible*, copyright © 1989 National Council of the Churches of Christ in the United States of America. Used by permission. All rights reserved.

Quotation from "Stations on the Way to Freedom" reprinted with the permission of Scribner, a Division of Simon & Schuster, Inc., from *Ethics* by Dietrich Bonhoeffer, translated from the German by Neville Horton Smith. Copyright © 1955 by SCM Press Ltd. Copyright © 1955 by Macmillan Publishing Company. All rights reserved.

Library and Archives Canada Cataloguing in Publication

Farris, James, 1923-, author
    Theological times : an autobiographical review / James Farris.

Includes bibliographical references.
Issued in print and electronic formats.
ISBN 978-0-9947721-0-7 (bound).—ISBN 978-0-9947721-1-4 (paperback).—
ISBN 978-0-9947721-2-1 (ebook)

1. Theology. 2. Farris, James, 1923-. I. Title.

BR118.F37 2015	230	C2015-903261-X
		C2015-903262-8

Mosa Press
www.mosapress.ca

Contents

Foreword	ix
Introduction	1
Words and the Word	7
Remembering Nineteenth-Century Theologians	23
Karl Barth	35
Bonhoeffer: Prophet and Martyr	45
Interpretation of Texts	59
Interpreting Stories: Theirs and Ours	73
From Cosmos to Quanta	97
After Words	115
Appendix: A Path for Religious Dialogue	125
About the Author	139

*Dedicated to my students,
who have taught me.*

Foreword

Having prepared this autobiographical study using a personal signature, it seems fitting to offer an accompanying outline biography with attributions and names attached. I was born at Glencoe, Ontario in 1923, the year that *Time* began, in the farm home of middle-aged parents, Charles and Euphemia. Family life held church and moral standards in central position, without being oppressive.

My mother had taught for twelve years in the iconic one-room school with ten grades. My own formal primary education followed the pattern with one teacher, the devout Mildred Robinson, who never neglected the daily prayer or award of stars for Scripture memorization. My father, who had been a pioneer homesteader in Western Canada, tutored me in a strenuous interlude as a very junior farmer.

When I went up to Western University, Professor Alison Johnson, a leading process philosopher, advised that I extend my intended program by a year, insisting that rigorous academics would accord with intended church ministry. Later, at Knox College, Principal Bryden was of like mind in my preparation for ordination in the Presbyterian Church in Canada in 1950.

In later graduate studies at New College, Edinburgh, Professor Tom Torrance became my volunteer director, facilitating arrangements giving me leave and introductions for research in Switzerland. On the way I had the benefit of a month's residence in Bonn at the home of Professor Hermann Schlingensiepen and his wife, who provided me with gracious introduction to German language and culture.

At Basel, Professor Oscar Cullmann, as housefather of Alumneum residence, showed kindly interest that included occasional letter exchanges until his death nearly forty years later. At the University I attended lectures from the two Karls, Jaspers and Barth, delivered in adjoining rooms from contrasting existential viewpoints. My final academic enrolment, postdoctoral, transpired later at Union Theological Seminary, New York where I was mentored by a fellow Canadian, Professor James Smart.

My most engaged learning experience unfolded in a ten-year teaching mission in Guyana and Jamaica. There I had direct encounter with Hindu and Muslim religions and the growing pains of the independence movement. The times afforded me substantial involvement in establishment of the United Theological College of the West Indies.

My longest teaching assignment extended to a quarter century of teaching philosophical theology and world religions at Knox College where I retain emeritus standing. Post-Vatican II experience favoured development of the ecumenical Toronto

School of Theology. In my specialty the regular appearance of Jesuits and their female counterparts in the classroom markedly raised the bar and challenge of ecumenical discourse. During these years I enjoyed sabbatical opportunity for study visits to the United Kingdom, Germany, and S.E. Asia, and a semester of teaching at the University of Otago, New Zealand.

ACKNOWLEDGEMENTS

The most intimate and personal encouragement has been that of my wife, Jean, in urging the completion of these studies for publication. I am particularly indebted to Dr. Peter Denton and Dr. Michael Farris for encouragement and editorial assistance. Other friends who have been readers and helpful commentators include Dr. Andrew Fullerton, Rev. Raymond Drennan, and Dr. Willoughby Lemen. I am also grateful to Donald Burnett, who has provided invaluable technical assistance.

Introduction

INTRODUCING A THEOLOGICAL STUDY IN terms suggestive of journal entries may evoke a negative reaction in some minds. This reaction may stem from the fact that major religions have been perceived to rise in very ancient times and appear untouched by temporality. Their language and rituals sound intimations of eternity. The devotional sanctity associated with religious persons and texts speaks of continuity.

When a religious community has progressed to the point of displaying a distinct culture one can discern features of the iconic debate between the ancient Greek philosophers: Parmenides the champion of permanence, and Heraclitus the prophet of change. The latter is credited with the proverb that "you cannot step twice into the same river"; a second footprint will be different. With reference to a living religion, the Heraclitian theme ought surely to be honoured.

Those of us professing faith inspired by the Hebrew and Christian scriptures are without excuse if we are resistant to the very concept of change in the language and conduct of our pieties. The history of Israel and the Church covers a long trail of transitions. It traces Abraham's wanderings toward the Land of Promise. It depicts the progress of the Tribes of Israel through conquest, serfdom, royal kingship, exile, and prophetic tuition in support of the promise. In Christian tradition the decisive historic moment is the in-breaking of Jesus the Christ whose transforming mission was long regarded as the twofold marker for measuring epochs of time, past and future.

The design of these pages is to review distinctive elements in the historical unfolding of Christian theological reflection in the nineteenth and twentieth centuries. The reflections have been those of an individual entering his tenth decade who has spent over forty years in theological research and teaching, the latter exercised during a decade in Caribbean countries and more than a quarter-century in Canada. An exhaustive historical account is not being attempted but a report on those issues that specially drew his attention. It must be admitted that many other views and further reviews are needed. Speaking here as reviewer, it is my belief that historical insight and benefit may be gained from following the steps of a pilgrim on the pathway of faith seeking understanding.

The unfolding of Christian theology over an expanse of time bears witness to the eschatological thrust of the Gospel in reflection and proclamation. The call to faith in Jesus Christ is a summons to live in light of the end times, involved in the service of the Kingdom. My own Reformed tradition has insisted on regarding the Church through the transit of time as *semper reformanda* (always reforming). The modern ecumenical movement has seen the Christian centre shift from its heartland in Europe to North America, and now to the south, or third world, to gain greater membership and evangelical appeal.

Change, however, has not been conspicuously directive in church polity or architectural symbolism. The sundial and analogical clockface have been prominent features at the parish centre, although not always in step with the pace of environing society. That remark recalls a visit to the beautiful Cathedral of Notre Dame in Strasbourg, France in which one transept is devoted to supporting the large astronomical clock. The feature was erected in the fourteenth century and restored in the nineteenth. Twice daily for six centuries a door on the clock balcony has opened to reveal a mechanized march around the tower by the twelve Apostles in effigy. The irony in this vignette relates to the history of Strasbourg and its environs. It was long a German cultural centre, but in the last two centuries its language and sovereignty alternated between Germany and France several times. Yet after high noon and midnight the apostolic march has continued, unmoved by the political and cultural strains engrossing the city, not to mention the declining religious presence in post-revolutionary France.

A millennium before the first Strasbourg clock, Saint Augustine wrestled philosophically over the meaning of time. In his *Confessions* he pondered the mystery.[1] Past time and future time figure so largely in

---

1. Saint Augustine, *Confessions*, Book XI, trans. R.S. Pine-Coffin (New York: Penguin, 1961).

the Christian story, yet he was mindful that past time has slipped away from us, the present is but an instant, and the future beyond our grasp. After a somewhat playful musing over the problem Augustine finally came to a resolution in essentially psychological terms that he found satisfying. He concluded that past times and future times are united in our experience as an eternal moment. This resolution was a denial that there is any substantive break in time's passage between past and future. Rather than being a mere bridge extended between two alien shores, time bears the weight of a dynamic relation between memory and hope. The threefold present embraces not only the *extension* of time but also, and perhaps more importantly according to Augustine, the *distension* of time. The sense of the latter term could be conveyed by the image of the distension of the womb in preparation for the birthing of offspring.

A more sophisticated appreciation of Augustine's insight has been voiced in modern times. Bertrand Russell, who would have had little sympathy with Augustine's doctrinal theology, nonetheless credited him with a philosophical breakthrough in his concept of time. Of this he wrote: "Clearly a very able theory, deserving to be seriously considered.... it is a great advance over anything to be found on the subject in Greek philosophy."[2]

Further in the twentieth century, an echo of

---

2. Bertrand Russell, *History of Western Philosophy* (London: Allen and Unwin, 1946), 374.

Augustine's image of time's distension appears in Henri Bergson's characterization of time as *duration,* a term that suggests an eventful, momentous unfolding. From France also has come a significant contemporary philosophical view of temporality. In his trilogy, *Time and Narrative,* the religious philosopher, Paul Ricœur, distinguished two aspects of time, cosmic time and human time.[3] Universal or cosmic time is mainly lost in the spatial and temporal void. Human time is time reified through human consciousness and modulated through our narrative capability, whether rhetorical or textual.

It is through narrative that we give ourselves a history. Taking the model of psychoanalysis, Ricœur states that we are able to see how the story of a life comes to be constituted through a series of rectifications applied to previous narrative. In the same way, the history of a people, a collectivity, or institution proceeds from the series of corrections that new historians bring to their predecessors' descriptions and interpretations. He instances the point by considering biblical testimony, observing that the historical community called *the Jewish people* has drawn its ideality and its identity from the rectification and reconception of those texts which it had itself produced.

In the following pages we will review narrative expositions of theological reflection and debate that have been prominent in the nineteenth and twentieth

---

3. Paul Ricœur, *Time and Narrative*, 3 vols. (Chicago: University of Chicago Press, 1989).

centuries. The narratives selected will in some measure represent a series of attempted rectifications of preceding ones. The fact that most of the narratives will be in German voice reflects a timely judgment about the theological discourse of a particular period.

In present time our theological narratives should be presented in the full light of encounter with great living religions other than our own. The times also require that we discourse in light of the cosmological picture to which we have been introduced by modern science, a picture which places us, theologians and others, in an evolving dynamic universe in which we are both part and participant. As subjects whose vocation is to bring our times to consciousness and speech, as Paul Tillich affirmed, we have a heavy commission to speak the truth with ultimate concern. Our being alive within the flow of time situates us in both the sphere of moral responsibility and the sphere of spiritual waiting.

Words and the Word

THE THREE GREAT RELIGIONS EMANating from the Middle East – Judaism, Christianity and Islam – are strongly textual. Their spoken and written words are formative and performative, descriptive and prescriptive. When Muhammad referred to followers of the earlier religions as *People of the Book* he was describing his own folk as well. Within the Christian community and its cultural network our self-awareness and our cosmology have been formed by texts. With historical and emotive ties to the Hebrew scriptures, Christians are also beneficiaries of the literary heritage and conceptuality of Greek and Roman language and culture which focused the intellectual framework employed by the early church fathers. By virtue of that fact, we have access to a large body of writings that informed a movement toward primitive natural science and the breakthrough to modernity that we name the Enlightenment.

In the literary field, Canadian critic Northrop Frye has prompted us to appreciate the subliminal function of the Bible that underlies our literary usage in the languages of Christian Europe. His thesis is highlighted in his widely read book, *The Great Code,* which instances language patterns, especially in English, that support his view.[1] It is clear that many writers and speakers employ terms that reflect religious ideas and values that they fail to identify or acknowledge. Such insensitivity illustrates the ambiguity that is endemic in our appropriation of language.

Our ability to do things with words, modulated by a broad range of grammatical inflections, including especially mood and tense, is a distinct advantage humans possess over other species. We are able to create language qualified by a great variety of myth, metaphor and symbol. Problematically, however, we can both inform and obstruct understanding in our complex language use. The prevalence of advertising and propaganda spin requires us constantly to exercise a hermeneutics of suspicion.[2] The apostle James pointed out the profane peril affecting both our address of God and other persons (James 3:5). The interpretation of scripture and our prophetic task requires the discerning use of language. The long history of doctrinal reflection and affirmation in the Christian church has been characterized by divisions of discernment and judgment – divisions that have defined both orthodoxies and heresies.

Continuing into the twenty-first century, some

---

1. Northrop Frye, *The Great Code* (Toronto: Harcourt, 1982).
2. Paul Ricœur, *Freud and Philosophy* (New Haven: Yale University Press, 1970).

Christian churches remain entangled in controversies that stem from ignorance or from literal interpretations of religious texts that support a rigid and militant fundamentalism. Some historic Christian communions with a respected tradition of learning and strong leadership in promoting social justice are nevertheless tearing themselves apart in sectarian fashion and are the object of adverse judgment and demeaning rhetoric voiced freely in agnostic and atheist critiques.

It is lamentable that the most divisive issue encountered in major Christian communities of late has been the subject of homosexuality during a time when many social ills and moral dilemmas on a global scale urgently call for thoughtful attention. Debate on this issue inevitably becomes a battle in biblical interpretation. (Most quoted in conservative riposte are verses found in Leviticus 18:22, 20:13; and Romans 1:26–27.)

In historical perspective, at the time of the Levitical writings, the tribes of Israel were passing through a period of moral and spiritual searching to find a firm basis for political and social order while facing large potential predator enemies. Their sense of mission was formed from the dream of Abraham that from the fruit of his loins would be born a great nation with a divinely ordered destiny. In that era there was no knowledge of the genetic contribution of the woman to human progeny. At best she was credited with being a seedbed. Homosexuality presented an obvious threat to family and racial survival through wasting of the sacred seed. Concern over injury to the genital organ was further evidence of the prime responsibility vested in the male. The fact that lesbianism is not proscribed in the Hebrew scriptures and its presence ignored, suggests that it was not seen as a problem, this in spite of the fact that is was surely known to exist. Saint Paul, in approaching this issue remained within the patriarchal stance, notwithstanding the fact that he supported equality of the sexes in respect to the evangel and to pastoral concern (Galatians 3:28).

The foregoing hermeneutical note is not intended as a model for all textual problems relating to the Bible and social criticism. It has been instanced to point to the deplorable fact that the long history of higher critical reading of the Bible has not educated a large section of Christian leadership away from a literal reading that ignores scientific and technological gains in linguistics and historical study of cultures. Paul Ricœur made the helpful proposal that when reference is made to the biblical *witness* the legal metaphor should be extended to regard its content as *testimony*. Testimony is normally advanced in court to be viewed as information or opinion that is contingent and limited by the personal circumstance and general knowledge of the one giving the testimony. The testimonies rising from religious experience may often be interpreted as coming from the mouth of God, but earnest faith should wait upon guidance of the divine Spirit and a trial of such testimonies before coming to judgment. (It is worthy of note that Karl Barth, theologian of the Word, commonly referred to the scriptures as *testimony*.)

Similarly, in the age of gender equality now observed by major populations of the Western world, it remains a stumbling block to a positive image of the Church that in the major part of its global institutions women may not advance to the highest office and responsibility in ecclesiastical roles. In theological studies it has become common to find women, who were denied ordination, pursuing academic advancement to the level where they may serve as teachers of male postulants. This is anomalous in an era when patriarchy has been largely overcome in political, scientific, literary and social institutional life. The oft-quoted fact that Jesus chose to itinerate with twelve males ought surely to be seen as reflecting cultural proprieties of the first century rather than dominical warrant for all time.

Aside from cultural phenomena of patriarchy and sexual orientation, it has been the broad impact of modern science and technology from Copernicus onward that has been the main feature of the battle between modernists and fundamentalists. The military metaphor remains still in play, however, despite the fact that a significant nineteenth-century historical study assumed that armistice was possible. In *A History of the Warfare of Science with Theology in Christendom,* A.D. White chronicled issues such as Darwin's discovery and advancement of evolutionary theory as though it were a battle of the past.[3] Yet the theory remains still troubling to many conservative minds.

---

3. A.D. White, *A History of the Warfare of Science with Theology in Christendom* (New York: Appleton, 1896).

I confronted repeatedly the anguished disorientation of students unable to accept the evidence for evolutionary development of life forms. The continuing attempt of creationists to overturn the evidence has no prospect of convincing the scientific community. Scientists remain similarly unimpressed with intelligent design arguments. On Planet Earth, and extended throughout the universe, contingent events too often make untenable the argument in support of an original harmony of phenomena within a young Earth. Prospective events such as the Day of Rapture and state of the *left behind* fall outside any concept of empirical historical unfolding.

Apart from the creationists, most contenders for the faith are unlikely to challenge the prevailing weight of science with the kind of projects that seem to excite the hard Christian right. The fact that the latter still lay claim to intellectual respect probably owes much to the impact of scholarly conservative publications produced during the first three decades of the twentieth century and circulated widely throughout North America. Wealthy fundamentalists in the United States underwrote the costs and over three million copies of the twelve-volume series were distributed between 1910 and 1915. (Copies of the booklets, entitled *The Fundamentals*, were found, for example, in the library residue of my great-uncle who had ministered among U.S. Presbyterians.)

As a teenager I read many of these, which contained articles written by scholars of the U.K. as well as North

America. The studies embraced doctrinal themes related to five basic affirmations of the New Testament concerning Christ: his virgin birth, divinity, atoning death, bodily resurrection, and promised return. The claim of biblical inerrancy was prominent throughout the series, a position strongly advanced by Benjamin Warfield and Charles Hodge of Princeton. It was not clear then, nor in current use, how the term *inerrancy* should be understood, whether in terms of fidelity to history, to science, or to the author's consistency in use of terms. Conservative adherence to these teachings was in marked contrast even then with current modernistic preaching and teaching. The modernist label was attached to such notables as Harry Emerson Fosdick, the pastor of Riverside Church in New York City. With him and his peers, questions concerning the truth of the Bible had probably ceased to be an urgent enquiry, but the Bible's contents would be mined for concepts and metaphors with moralist and homiletical potential.

Fairness would suggest that modernists should acknowledge the spiritual conviction and uplift that accompanied the extensive reading of the Bible, a practice that continued throughout the period. This was furthered by the agency of the Bible Societies which have made the Bible widely available for study and meditation without commentary. Before becoming a candidate for ministerial training, I had read the Bible twice in totality. As with most of the general readership, my own view of the cosmos, the moral order, and the spiritual destiny of humankind had been shaped with considerable definiteness. That kind of reading had yielded both conviction and hope through many generations and sparked more than one great spiritual awakening. In meeting the test of mature experience and education, however, the results have been less impressive. I still recall my shock when in a first-year classics lecture the professor casually commented: "Of course if Solomon were alive today he would immediately be clapped into jail on a charge of polygamy." I was prompted to recognize that many programs of Christian education have tended to romanticize the stories and to sanctify individual characters out of some pious intention. Unfortunately, interpretive exegesis outside the tuition of home and church school is not commonly found in the wider Christian community.

LOGICAL ANALYSIS

The great advance of scientific enterprise in the nineteenth century was founded upon the empirical method propounded by John Locke and David Hume. The allied advances through industrialization resulted in improved living standards and social development. By the early years of the twentieth century, a shift in intellectual interests turned from focusing on material conditions of life to exploring the limits of knowledge for understanding the universe and the human intellect itself. Einstein pressed the boundaries of our knowledge of the physical universe with his probing of the space/time relation. In the same temporal frame came a serious attempt to critique the legitimacy of the language we employ in communicating facts and ideas. This was a strenuous move in the philosophical tradition that had produced such thoroughgoing attempts at securing clarity of thought and utterance as Immanuel Kant's *Critique of Pure Reason*.

The renewed rigour in critiquing language use in the twentieth century is associated with the work of Ludwig Wittgenstein and colleagues of the Vienna Circle. They were intent to show that much widely used vocabulary and related forms of speech referred to metaphysical entities for which no empirical test was possible. It was claimed that a statement such as "God is good" cannot be verified by empirical investigation, and is to be regarded as meaningless. Wittgenstein urged strict economy of speech based on the dictum "whereof we cannot speak, thereof we must be silent." He was convinced that whatever we have to say is capable of being said clearly. In his 1921 book, *Tractatus Logico-Philosophicus*, he set out seven major assertions, accompanied by substatements, which he presumed would provide the framework for speech requirements in any situation we might encounter.[4] The book became in effect the source book for the philosophical movement termed *logical positivism*. A major

---

4. Ludwig Wittgenstein, *Tractatus Logico-Philosophicus* (New York: Routledge, 1981).

implication of this radical positivism was to remove ethical concepts and principles from discussion, leaving moral behaviour subject to emotional pressures and occasional preference.

In an undergraduate class I was introduced to logical positivism through one of its most popular exponents, A.J. Ayer, in his book *Language, Truth, and Logic*.[5] It seemed to some of us then that the great heritage of philosophical reasoning on which we were spending so much effort was being written off as a waste of time. From scholars writing in this vein, the *verification principle* became normative. The principle stipulated that the grounds for advancing a scientific conclusion were in effect the same as those used for disproving it. Based on this principle, the negative outlook tends to have the advantage where a truth question is in contention. The issues are likely first to be dealt with negatively, as problem rather than promise.

It was not long before the constraints of the logical positivist position came to be seen as too limiting. Too many value judgments come into focus even when we are judging simple matters of fact. Metaphorical and imaginative terms, which cannot meet the empirical challenge, abound in our language and play an important part in our ability to say things clearly. Drawing exploratory word pictures is a common device of scientists both in research and in didactic purpose.

---

5. A.J. Ayer, *Language, Truth and Logic* (London: Victor Gollancz, 1936).

In provisional emplotment of solutions to problems, and in description of the solutions, the language may inevitably border on the metaphysical. In the broad scheme of things the development of *points of view* may depend upon first holding a *world view* in order to position facts or events on a scale of values or importance. Terms of comparison and judgment do not easily lend themselves to empirical test. Simple connectives (such as *rather, further* and *moreover*) are functions of ordinary language and are imponderables that cannot be checked for objectivity. Obviously it was the language of poetry that was most impoverished under the constraints of the verification principle.

By the end of World War II, the influence of Wittgenstein had declined, although modifications of his views continued to be important in England. After the War, during which Wittgenstein had volunteered for war service, his teaching at Cambridge became relatively informal and reached the public only with the posthumous publication of his *Philosophical Investigations.*[6] In the latter volume he turned away from the sparse use of language and the univocal meanings assigned to it in the *Tractatus,* giving the terms of ordinary language a decidedly equivocal role. He came to the conclusion that words have meaning only in the use to which they are put. The implication of the language-in-use principle meant that lexical meaning could vary by subject and occasion. This, of course,

---

6. Ludwig Wittgenstein, *Philosophical Investigations* (Oxford: Blackwell, 1945).

had long been recognized in the great lexicons such as the *Oxford English Dictionary* where multiple examples of accepted usage are listed. In many fields, writers began to move toward employing ordinary language in terms suited to subject matter. In theology, the change meant that books were being published under the banner of biblical theology where the source of reflection was the scriptural text, rather than themes related to philosophical or linguistic analyses. Translations of the Bible thus increasingly reflected ordinary language.

With attention declining from strict reference to objects of knowledge, the emphasis shifted to the phenomenon of language itself. The philosophy of linguistic analysis tended to become primordial to the issue of what is said. The structure of language in itself becomes an issue when, for example, one considers the nature of the tautology, so commonly employed in mathematical and legal definitions, in contrast with terms of contingent historical or scientific description. The colour or tonality of language is at issue when one uses similar vocabulary, but with differing intent, as in the case of describing a deathbed scene distinct from describing a terminal pathology.

In the twentieth century a major contest developed in France between two ways of featuring the development and employment of language: that of the structuralists, associated with the thought of Ferdinand de Saussure; and that of the deconstructionists, associated with the thought of Jacques Derrida. (The contrast in outlooks has been reviewed in wide-ranging literature that we will not here explore.) In brief, the structuralists saw meaning in the recurrence of distinct forms in literature and social patterns that conveyed meaning simply by their consistent pattern of use or resonance – as, for example, in patriotic odes to one's country. In contrast, deconstructionists attempted to expose how many terms in common use needed to be stripped of an accumulated weight of meaning, such as those that may have been culturally relevant in patriarchal times, but are no longer so in a republican, egalitarian era. The issues raised by structuralism and deconstructionism have obvious relevance to theology, but will probably remain attached to aspects of linguistics rather than mentoring different philosophical or theological systems. In this study, the contributions of philosophers of language such as Rudolf Bultmann, Martin Heidegger and Paul Ricœur will be considered for their impact on hermeneutics relating to religious language.

Turning from language analysis, we consider theologies of the Word from the same era that offered meaning markedly different from meaning constrained by an empirical straitjacket. The theologies of the Word testified to revelatory disclosures informing the biblical heritage, apprehended in relational terms, rather than in the detachment that characterizes subject–object enquiry. Considered as a movement, these theologies came to be denominated as neo-orthodoxy. Its expressive features were more rhetorical and homiletical than philosophical. Its social and intellectual outlook was shaped largely in reaction to nineteenth-century historicism and idealism, as well as to the moral and spiritual rupture of the two great wars.

NEO-ORTHODOXY

Turning to a study of neo-orthodoxy after reviewing features of modernity involving science and language issues is justified because it was a movement that stood apart from the general current of its cultural environment. During the fifty years following the outbreak of World War I, neo-orthodoxy was principally a feature of German and Swiss theological discourse and church life that had little to do with the linguistic concerns that produced analytical philosophy in the English-speaking world. In the United Kingdom, it was probably the residue of the Oxford Movement that offered the more significant intellectual support for the Christian cause. In the United States the religious studies of William James and the developing Social Gospel movement had a positive impact on religious life quite apart from the pervasive fundamentalist/modernist debate. In Europe, as a whole, waning political idealism and rising optimistic social Darwinism constituted a broad cultural background.

It was theologians of Germany and Switzerland who provided the major evidence supporting the claim by Edinburgh theologian, H. R. McIntosh, that the nineteenth was the greatest century of Christian theology since the fourth.[7] And it was in reaction to that theological heritage that Karl Barth rose to eminence early in the twentieth century, leading in due course to estimates that he was the greatest theologian since Aquinas (or, in Reformed-speak, the greatest since Calvin). With early colleagues such as Eduard Thurneysen and Friedrich Gogarten supportive of his views, Barth launched an attack against the prevailing religious-historical theology and philosophical idealism that undergirded liberal modernism. I came to realize how intense was that negative reaction during a semester spent attending Barth's lectures on the fourth volume of his *Dogmatics* at the University of Basel. The experience coincided with the research I was doing in nineteenth-century theology while on graduate study leave from the University of Edinburgh.

The same period was remarkable for the theological leadership and publications by notable scholars who had been disciplined by the thought of the great century and were in differing modes of relation to it. The scholars identified below were those, with one exception, I had been able to encounter in the context of classroom or lecture experience. It is interesting to note how their birth dates clustered: Walter Bryden (1883); Rudolf Bultmann (1884); Karl Barth (1886); Paul Tillich (1886): John Baillie (1886); Eduard Thurneysen

---

7. Hugh Ross Mackintosh, *Types of Modern Theology: Schleiermacher to Barth* (London: Nisbet, 1937), 5.

(1888); Emil Brunner (1889); and Reinhold Niebuhr (1892). Of these men, Walter Bryden, my teacher and mentor at Knox College, first introduced me to the unfolding currents of European theology. Without direct contact with Karl Barth, he had come to similar criticism of post-Enlightenment liberal theology because it had failed to inspire or nurture him in his vocation as pastor, or later as teacher.[8] The passion of his commitment to upholding the revelatory Word, unencumbered with apologia, remains for me a memory held with sincere respect.

---

8. John Vissers, *The Neo-Orthodox Theology of W. W. Bryden* (Eugene, OR: Pickwick Publications, 2006).

Remembering Nineteenth-Century Theologians

A REVIEW OF NINETEENTH-CENTURY theologians identified in the following sketches is not simply prolegomena to understanding the origins of neo-orthodoxy. Their ruminations ended a long delay in offering a major studied Christian response to the Enlightenment and its challenge to traditional dogmas and religious practice. The efforts of nineteenth-century theologians to speak relevantly to the rising secularism of the educated classes were remarkably similar to the current homiletical and didactical task of communicating the Gospel within and outside church walls in the twenty-first century. With the decline in the impact and popularity of neo-orthodoxy by the mid-twentieth century, it became important to better understand the intellectual situation to which it had been reactive. During postdoctoral study at Union Theological Seminary, New York in 1959 I found that the faculty there were just catching up with neo-orthodoxy — and at the same time passing it by. I attended the first seminar they had ever offered on Karl Barth, which had only a sparse attendance. A senior faculty member at the same time, to another audience, was commenting on the changing situation in Europe and ended with his conclusion that "the new watchword in theology must be *forward to the nineteenth century!*"

For anyone proposing to take that temporal reversal seriously, an attempt must be made to understand the foundation and features of the earlier liberal theology, which may still have something to teach us. Karl Barth himself made the case for maintaining informed awareness of the teachings that he so heavily criticized. He wrote a major, detailed and balanced historical study under the title: *Protestant Thought from Rousseau to Ritschl.*[1] In the early nineteenth century the most eminent German theologian was Friedrich Schleiermacher (1768–1834). An indication of his scholarly rank may be signalled by the anecdote that Karl Barth, his stern critic, retrieved and restored a bust of Schleiermacher found in 1947 amidst the war ruins of the University of Bonn. As theologian, Schleiermacher's distinctive move was to place theology within a subjective psychological framework in which he considered religious consciousness to be situated. His intent was to rehabilitate religion from its embrace by cold rationalism. A Kantian in his re-

---

1. Karl Barth, *Protestant Thought from Rousseau to Ritschl* (New York: Harper & Brothers, 1959).

jection of metaphysical system, he was at the same time a romanticist in his undertaking to give theology its expression wholly from within subjective consciousness. He urged that we should do everything *with* religion rather than *from* religion as defined in the creeds. Proceeding religiously, his reflections constituted a major modern attempt to elaborate a natural theology. In outline his thought may be found in the volume *On Religion: Speeches to Its Cultured Despisers.*[2] Schleiermacher defined religion as the feeling of absolute dependence that we have in relation to God. His view of God had no place for the traditional five ways posed by Aquinas. All traditional doctrines that had been defined by the church he regarded as simply expressions of the religious consciousness. He maintained that "piety is the operation of God upon you by the operation of the world upon you," since God is immanent in the world.[3]

He believed that Christ, as God incarnate, should be perceived as model and guide for us, the ideal man. The human ideal was latent at Creation; but it became completely historical in Jesus. As the Christ, he redeems us by strengthening our God-consciousness. We are enabled to reach a state of perfection through the aid of the Spirit, conceived not as a being from beyond, but as the common spirit engendered within the community of the church.

---

2. Friedrich Schleiermacher, *On Religion: Speeches to Its Cultured Despisers* (London: Kegan Paul, 1893).
3. Ibid., 9.

The romanticist idealism described in psychological terms by Schleiermacher was expanded by Georg Hegel (1770–1831) to embrace a radical absolute idealism achieved by rational reflection engendered within human minds. In fact, Hegel believed that the world of human experience and all material entities is derived wholly from the creativity of rational mind, rather than being based upon material objectivity. He employed a triadic form of thought through which he would demonstrate that wherever opposition arises between two ideas or propositions, the perplexity is overcome by resort to a higher thought that embraces and comprehends the lower ones. The ability to recognize opposition is by that very recognition the overcoming of opposition. Opposition thought is opposition overcome. From problems in the family to statist conflict, harmony can be achieved through taking thought.

It has commonly been noted that the Hegelian ideal was inverted in Marxist/Leninism to demonstrate absolute materialism. The capitalizing of labour and resolving of class conflict through the dictatorship of the proletariat was perceived as basic for management of industry and wealth through a communal system of planning and enforcement. The absolutist design was to bring into being a materialist utopia.

In theological terms, which remained a vital element in Hegel's system, he used his triadic reasoning to elucidate the meaning of the Trinity. God is perceived as transcendent being, moving out of foundational selfhood to appear historically in Christ. The potential dualism is overcome by the all-embracing Spirit; thus making the third person of the Trinity the absolute form of deity. Hegel regarded Christianity as the ideal religion, while other religions are movements in process of supervening primitive tribal states to gain more intelligible forms. The Hegelian F.C. Baur applied the same methodology to ecclesiastical history. He envisioned a universal church beyond any existing claims to catholicity, anticipating the much later ecumenical accomplishments. In more common piety, the idealist impulse could be seen in optimistic claims that things were getting better every day in every way. In the U.S. there was a strong trace of idealism in the social gospel movement. Later in time, political idealism during the scourge of war would be manifest in the promotion of Woodrow Wilson's Fourteen Points, and in the formation of the League of Nations. The development of globalization in economic and political terms in later times could be viewed as a fading afterglow of the Hegelian vision.

Among theologians influenced by Hegel, David Friedrich Strauss (1808–74) made the greatest impact on Biblical studies. His *Life of Jesus* (1835) belonged to a genre of historical reconstructions developed as illustrations of an ideal. He held the view that most moral and religious narratives of history are informed by myths, a concept that has been prominent in twentieth-century New Testament study. He considered that the broad historical extension of the Hebrew and

Christian religions beyond their native soil was due to the fact that, in greater part, their myths are rooted in universal ideas.

The fact that many features of the life of Jesus are uncertain was not critical for Strauss who was not presenting him as a supernatural being but as an exemplar of the potentiality of the human race, namely that all could become Christians. In sum, he viewed the religion of Jesus as a model that took us away from an external historical religion to one that was uniquely personal and spiritual.

In *The Old and the New Faith*, Strauss criticized the religious tradition of separating time and eternity, soul and body. In that respect he welcomed Darwin's theory of evolution because it eliminated the need to assume an external divine architect of the world. He regarded the fundamental character of religion to be wish fulfilment. With his contemporary, Ludwig Feuerbach, he believed that the personality ascribed to God is but the personality of humans projected, with our ideals and aspirations flung upon the clouds.

A decided change from the subjectivism and individualism that had been dominant in Schleiermacher and the Hegelians was found in the turn to social and historical Christianity in the thought of Albrecht Ritschl (1822–89). His aim was to ground religion in the life world, presenting Christianity as an historical religion, the medium through which we know God. In spite of having made this claim, he did not propose that we should depend absolutely upon historical action. The test of the validity of the Christian religion rests on its ability to give the believer a sense of mastery over the world. In this sense "the justification of Christian doctrine depends upon an immanent human norm of value."[4]

In value terms we are to esteem Jesus as a model of moral and spiritual leadership. Jesus embodies for us the religious value of God. In the historical unfolding of the Kingdom of God the meaning and value of the Christian life is disclosed. Ethically directed action represents our highest good. This development of an historical approach to Christianity implied that it could be studied and described historically in comparative relationship with other historical religions. Eventually this approach appealed to a broad section of philosophical and religious scholars whose group identity came to be known as the Religious-Historical School *(Religionsgeschichtliche Schule)*.

Prominent among the members of this school was Ernst Troeltsch (1865–1923), who insisted that the comparative study of religion ought not to be pursued narrowly in the interest of faith, but should be studied simply with historical objectivity like all other objects of study which are relative and conditional. He held the view that the aptitude of Europeans and Americans for the study of Christianity should not justify its being treated as a universal religion for all races

---

4. W. J. S. Farris, "The Concept of Divine Immanence in the Theology of the Nineteenth Century," (Ph.D. thesis, University of Edinburgh, 1954), 209.

and cultures. With his colleague at Heidelberg, Max Weber, he gave wide-ranging attention to the sociological features of the church in its historical setting.

In historical sequence, we can trace the interests and objectives of the Religious-Historical School coming to fruition in the widespread establishment of departments of religious studies in North American universities in the periods following both of the world wars. The non-confessional and academically objective character of these establishments can be illustrated by the rueful admission that a Catholic colleague and I shared one Sunday afternoon while attending a conference of the American Academy of Religion. We registered the fact that members had been discussing religion all weekend without any time devoted to religious exercises in a devotional setting!

Arguably, the most influential church historian of the nineteenth century, and one whose influence extended well into the following century, was Adolph von Harnack (1851–1930). His seven-volume *History of Dogma* continues to be an authoritative resource in use today. His importance extended well beyond the academy, as he was an advisor to contemporaries in the political domain. In a photograph of 1913 he appears in the company of Kaiser Wilhelm II of Germany and his political and domestic staff. The occasion was the unfolding of a new military preparedness planning session by the imperial government. It is not surprising then that Harnack was among a group of theological professors who signed a statement of support for the aims of the Central Powers upon the outbreak of war in August 1914. The opposing allies of course enlisted comparable support from their religious communities. In Harnack's case, however, this patriotic support continued through and beyond the War. He continued after the War to be an advisor to the Weimar Republic. From neutral Switzerland Karl Barth had been deeply disillusioned by the militarist stance taken by several of his former revered teachers. It was only at a 1923 religious conference that Barth and Harnack met again and the two men shook hands.

As a footnote to my research in nineteenth-century theology, which had related principally to Germany, I have to report that I came to appreciate that the tragedy of the Great War mounted a greater cultural shock in Germany than within the alliance of its enemies. The important title by Barbara Tuchman, *The Proud Tower: A Portrait of the World Before the War, 1890–1914* gave major attention to the eminence of German letters and arts in the period leading to the catastrophe.[5] For three generations scholars in many disciplines, and especially in religion and philosophy, had been coming to German universities for advanced graduate study. Barth's disappointment in his teachers notwithstanding, I learned that his was not the prevailing view of all his theological contemporaries. In Bonn I came to know well a seasoned professor of theology who was a wounded veteran of the Great War

---

5. Barbara Tuchman, *The Proud Tower: A Portrait of the World Before the War, 1890–1914* (London: Macmillan, 1966).

with close family roots in the old Germany and its political class. One day in discussion with him about the two wars and his own role as a member of the Confessing Church that had caused him to suffer under the Nazis, he suddenly reverted to the Great War and said in a clear voice: "But that was a just war." To my surprise, he did not offer to qualify the judgment.

I had to reflect that, a century ago, the option of the just war was still a subject for serious ethical debate. I was led to picture my friend as a young man undertaking studies to become a clergyman who was caught up in the passion of a Christian society committed to making the world safe for Christian civilization. This was a call heard in the West as well but probably not as clearly when clothed in terms of the slogan *to make the world safe for democracy.* The role of defender of the faith for Germans was pursued with the consciousness that a principal opponent was France, which in the post-revolutionary era had largely become humanist and hostile to organized religion.

Harnack contributed a piece to a German religious journal in 1915 in which he wrote with wounded sorrow, if not surprise, about the terrible hatred *(furchtbar Hass)* which opposing states had unleashed against the German Empire and people. In Germany the chaplaincy was heavily supported and in the critical war year of 1917 the populace, both Catholic and Protestant, marked the 400th anniversary of the Reformation with festive celebrations. The memorial plaques in historic German churches are heavily inscribed to the dead of the Great War who fought for *Gott und Vaterland.* The kind of piety that these memorials reflect is seen in the simple hand linking during grace at table that remains common in Christian homes. A Dutch clergy friend once commented on that piety in reporting the experience of a cousin who had been a maid in the exiled Kaiser's household at Doorn. She said it was Wilhelm's practice to alarm the staff at 6 AM and to summon them to gather for family prayers at 7 AM.

Karl Barth

THE EARLIER BRIEF REFERENCE TO Karl Barth calls for major amplification in recognition of the dominant role he played in setting the course of Protestant theology during the first half of the twentieth century. Revisiting the theological formation Barth experienced at the feet of some of his theological forebears seemed a necessary approach to introducing his radical turn away from it.

The turning came during his renewed concentration on study of the Scriptures during the Great War. Concerning this time he testified that he had encountered a "strange new world within the Bible" (1916). The discovery was made in fellowship and friendship with Eduard Thurneyson who, years later, would be his pastor at the Basel Cathedral. The torment of spirit Barth experienced as he sought to carry out his pastoral ministry in the Swiss town of Safenwil can be sensed from his foreword to the second edition of his study of the Epistle to the Romans. Confessing his inability to understand and interpret the scriptures as he would like, he laid the blame on his experience at the university which had not taken him beyond a certain "awe in the presence of history."

Among his teachers, he might have excepted from such critique Wilhelm Herrmann of Marburg, of whom he later spoke favourably regarding views held in common. By coincidence my *Doktorvater*, John Baillie, was also a student at Marburg at the same time as Barth. The two held mainly contrary views through most of their remaining careers. Barth became increasingly critical of the philosophical and historical emphases in the prevailing scholarship. In his struggle to obtain guidance he found the existentialist approach attractive for its dialectical relational mode of thought. His reading included the works of the Jewish philosopher, Martin Buber, who later in 1923 published the seminal volume, *I and Thou*, with its turn away from objective description to emphasize the priority of personal relation. Buber regarded personal address, which brings the speaker and the other person or thing into a dialectical relationship, to be the kind of knowing whereby we encounter God. In thus embracing God, the lines of relationship run throughout the entire experienced world.

Undoubtedly it was the Danish existentialist, Søren Kierkegaard, who exerted the greater influence on Barth. His view of God as the Wholly Other, unreachable by a chain of reasoning and accessible only by a leap of faith, became foundational for Barth in his dialectical stage. He was in agreement with Kierkegaard that the rational search leads only to despair because ideas cannot remove consciousness of sin and bring inner peace. In faith we learn to live with the absurd and the paradoxical, especially the state of trusting our soul's eternal salvation to something historical, that being the presence and action of God in the historic Christ. Faith means accepting historical uncertainty with passionate inwardness. Such a focus was supported by Kierkegaard with the declaration (found in his *Concluding Unscientific Postscript to the Philosophical Fragments*) that "subjectivity is truth." Being a subject, God can be apprehended only in subjective inwardness, and addressed only relationally. The condition for knowing God in this manner must be renewed in each generation, as there is no objective capital of faith to be handed on. Before God we are constantly in the position of having to respond to an either/or decision concerning aspects of Christian belief or action.

As Barth proceeded in his dogmatic reflections, he eventually moved away from Kierkegaard as he came to sense that existentialism was tending to become a system of belief attracting party loyalty. In similar vein, Barth would himself later attract a number of convinced disciples, which led him self-deprecatingly to disavow being a Barthian. He avoided engaging in interpretation (hermeneutics) in support of his views of the Bible and theological works. This could have meant importing philosophical and cultural ideas from outside the experience of faith in Jesus Christ. It is somewhat surprising, however, to find the philosopher Hans-Georg Gadamer crediting Barth with undertaking a massive hermeneutical project. He wrote, "in his great work *Church Dogmatics* Karl Barth contributes to the hermeneutical problem explicitly nowhere and indirectly everywhere."[1]

He went on to show the contrast with Bultmann who did have an explicit program of interpretation based on demythologizing the New Testament. What Gadamer had in mind may well have been the observation that Barth supported his biblically based *Dogmatics* with interpretive testimony drawn from the entire history of Christian thought. Whether in positive or negative terms, the pages of the Dogmatics are weighted with massive footnotes conveying testimony to the Christian presence in history and its doctrinal formularies.

That testimony was pervasive in everything Barth wrote, including extensive correspondence as well as invitational lectures. The magnitude and scope of the *Dogmatics* is too intimidating for cursory review. I recall Professor G. T. Thompson, translator of Volume 1, being asked during class about the difference between the early and the later Barth. He responded aptly by raising his arms at a distance suggestive of the shelf space needed for the intervening volumes. In a foreword to a detailed introduction to his principal volumes Barth professed surprise that they had not only been read *in extenso* but also understood. This hint of

---

[1]. Hans-Georg Gadamer, *Truth and Method* (New York: Crossroad, 1985), 473.

his wry humour points to an aspect of the manner in which he engaged students and enquirers who made their pilgrimage to Basel.[2] Barth listened intently to others, in demonstration of the relational character of his approach to the knowing process. At alternate fortnightly seminars for French and English speakers, conducted in his family dining room, questions and comment were freely allowed. He urged us to move forward in the theological enterprise, warning us that he might at some future time be called a dangerous heretic. He once slapped his book *Dogmatics in Outline* while we were discussing it, saying that in its time it was the best he could do but we must strive to do better. He did not suggest that we try to write as much!

For Barth the centrality of Christ in the Gospel is apprehended in the decision of faith. It is not to be wrested from a long temporal account of the historical Jesus. This was an issue between Barth and his New Testament colleague, Oscar Cullman. While I was resident in the Alumneum in Basel where Cullman was house father, he one day suggested that I might find interest in his small book *Königsherrschaft Christi und Kirche im Neuen Testament.* He said that Barth commended him on this work stating that it was the best thing he had ever written, adding: "After that, Oscar, you could just as well have died." With a knowing look, Cullman noted, "That was before I wrote *Christ and Time.*" Cullman was of course a principal

---

2. Otto Weber, *Karl Barth's Church Dogmatics* (Philadelphia: Westminster Press, 1953), 10.

representative of biblical theologians who stressed the historicity of the revelation in Christ, looking to its fulfilment in the Kingdom of Christ. This distinguished them as members of the History of Salvation (*Heilsgeschictliche*) movement. They were in opposition to Barth, and to a greater extent to Bultmann, as well, given his insistence that there is not an extended history of revelation, but faith's decision arises in the moment of a revelatory encounter with Christ.

The essence of Barth's central doctrine of revelation and his rejection of natural theology may be discerned from his lecture of 1947 at the University of Bonn concerning the Christian understanding of revelation. Conservative evangelical scholars, who somewhat belatedly discovered Barth through appreciation of the biblical outlines of his theology, would be well advised to heed this lecture. In it, Barth made clear that although the revelation of God is to be encountered in the Bible, his regard for the Bible did not support what may be implied by the terms *infallibility* or *inerrancy*. He recognized that "the Bible is a collection of human documents. It was written by men in the language of men, at a definite time in human history and in a definite human situation."[3]

In spite of those limitations, he made his summary affirmation concerning the witness of the Bible as revelation: "We have interpreted revelation as the self-revelation of God, that is, as his revelation in Jesus Christ,

---

3. Karl Barth, *Against the Stream* (London: SCM Press, 1954), 221.

as the word that is spoken to us, that is given to us in the witness of Holy Scripture. Wherever revelation in the Christian sense is known and acknowledged, there the Christian Church is. The Church is the reality which arises and continues wherever the revelation of God in Jesus Christ has made itself known."[4]

Much of the postwar interest in Barth, especially in North America, was focused on his involvement with the Confessing Church and the political implications of the Barmen Confession, largely authored by Barth. His earlier association with Christian Socialism may have accounted for his relatively accommodating relation to Marxism. He maintained Cold War personal relationships and advisory roles with churches of Eastern Europe in situations where there had at least been no formal restriction against preaching the gospel message. Largely because of these relationships, conservative elements in Swiss society had become reserved in attitudes toward their leading theologian. Invitations to speak on radio became infrequent, and on the occasion of the Hungarian uprising in 1956, Barth's silence was met with pointed criticism. (I heard hints of such negative criticism while attending a gathering of local Reformed clergy in Basel.) During the same time, however, Barth developed a more congenial attitude toward ecumenicity, including active participation in the work of the World Council of Churches after Amsterdam 1948. With Vatican II and his visit to Rome, he developed a more favourable re-

---

4. Ibid., 225.

lation to Catholicism than he had earlier displayed in his criticism of Catholic philosophical theology.

By the early 1950s the impulse of neo-orthodoxy and biblical theology had begun to wane. In the company of students in Basel, many of them struggling in late-night partisan debate with disciples of Bultmann fresh from studies at Marburg, I could sense that an era was passing. I had felt the same way much earlier at Knox College when it seemed that student enthusiasm for a well-rehearsed pattern of neo-orthodox creed was being substituted for critical reflection. Another troubling issue was Barth's consignment of world religions to the status of idolatry. My dissatisfaction in that respect called for a new engagement with other religions when I went directly from graduate studies to minister in the Indo-Guyanese community of then-British Guiana, in communities comprised mainly of Hindu and Muslim immigrants.

There remains no doubt, however, that Barth's monumental works will be studied for years to come, with the balance that such time affords. Significantly, some of his chief critical peers have expressed tributes to his influence. One of these was my Doktorvater, John Baillie, of whom Barth warned me when I asked his advice relative to my pending thesis. He confided, "Baillie and I are two different animals (*zwei verschiedene Tieren*)."

In his Gifford Lectures, published posthumously, Baillie continued his critical debate with Barth, particularly on the grounds that his Christological focus had not sufficiently recognized the revelation of God in nature and history, including the history of Israel, or that of the manifold world religions. In a final chapter, however, entitled "Retrospect," Baillie attempted to clarify his relations with Barth in an extended tribute that ran as follows:

"I need not say that Dr. Barth is a great man and a very great theologian, because everybody knows it. He has changed the face of Protestant theology far more radically than any other theologian during my lifetime. He has also made more difference than anybody else in my own attempts at theologizing. Whatever the measure of our agreements or disagreements with him, we have all to reckon with him. I have often said that there can be no hopeful forward advance beyond his teaching, as I fervently hope there will be, if we attempt to go round it instead of through it. There are already many signs of a reaction toward a more liberal outlook, but it must be a liberalism which, while regaining some of the lost pre-Barthian ground, has been much chastened by the many valuable things he has taught us."[5] A student of both men cannot do less than express gratitude for the extension of their gifts.

A further personal note is in order because it casts a gentler light on some of the sterner debates that tend to be endemic in the theological guild. John Baillie may have brought more than one overseas student to his classroom because they had read his little classic:

---

5. John Baillie, *The Sense of the Presence of God* (London: Oxford, 1962), 254.

A Diary of Private Prayer. A prayer desk occupied a prominent position in his study. From a personal friend of Dr. Baillie I heard a first-hand account of his final hours. With death imminent, he telephoned Dr. Murdo Ewan MacDonald, then the Gaelic-speaking minister of Saint George's West Parish in Edinburgh, inviting him to call at his house. After greeting him on his arrival, Dr. Baillie asked if he would kindly lead in Gaelic prayer. Murdo Ewan expressed surprise since he had never heard the other man speak Gaelic. Baillie replied that he did not speak it but could understand well because his father prayed with his family in Gaelic, and he would like to hear it once again. The two got down at their chairs and had a season of prayer. When they returned to their feet, Dr. Baillie gravely thanked his guest and struggled back upstairs, not to descend again before his death two days later.

Bonhoeffer: Prophet and Martyr

DURING THE PERIOD SURROUNDING World War II the name of Dietrich Bonhoeffer ranked closely in theological importance with that of Karl Barth both in Europe and America. It was the political bearing of their reputations that ensured their continuing influence, leading in one case to statist extradition and in the other to martyrdom. Dietrich Bonhoeffer must be credited with the most radical hermeneutical proposal in twentieth-century theology. In the months prior to his execution by Nazi Germany on the grounds of treason, he wrote letters in which he proposed moving to a *religionless* Christianity. In fragmentary notes that he passed to his dialogue partner, Eberhard Bethge, he went well beyond views shared earlier with Barth in viewing religions as idolatrous expressions of humanistic values. He came to adopt a position calling for traditional patterns of religiosity to yield to a believing life in which the essence of Christianity would be expressed simply in prayer and righteous action.

Bonhoeffer's roots were in Lutheranism with its foundational doctrine of salvation by faith alone. In his final development, however, he laid paramount emphasis on ethics, which no doubt reflected the struggles of conscience he underwent in offending traditional values of patriotism toward the nation state. The most striking feature of his latest teaching was its call for a *worldly Christianity.*

Before detailing Bonhoeffer's revolutionary thinking it is helpful to review at some length the distinctive ways in which he encountered the world as scholar and churchman, as prisoner of conscience, and finally as twentieth-century Christian martyr. His heroic fame in the English-speaking world may well rest more on the homiletical resources his career offered than on his theology with its far-reaching implications,.

He did not leave behind a major doctrinal treatise, but instead created a readership after World War II that was inspired by his martyrdom and appealing personhood. The details following rely heavily on a recent historical publication by a former student friend of mine.[1]

Unlike many of the eminent theologians who were his teachers and colleagues Bonhoeffer did not come from a family with a strong religious pedigree. His family in Berlin enjoyed a rich culture, but his father, a noted psychiatrist, was probably surprised to find that, alone of his eight children, Dietrich became

---

1. Ferdinand Schlingensiepen, *Dietrich Bonhoeffer 1906–45,* trans. Isabel Best (London: T&T Clarke, 2010).

deeply committed to the study and vocation of Christian faith. At age sixteen he opted to enter theological studies in the University of Berlin.

Dietrich advanced quickly, completing a Ph.D. in theology at age twenty-one, and at age twenty-three a second habilitation doctorate qualifying him to teach in the university. In 1931 at age twenty-five he published two volumes: *The Cost of Discipleship* and *Life Together*, which were hailed by Barth as the work of a rising star in theological scholarship. They were the volumes that first introduced him to the Christian public in Europe and North America. Prior to his ordination as a Lutheran minister, he served during 1928–29 as pastoral assistant in an expatriate German parish in Barcelona. In 1930–31 he entered a year of studies at Union Theological Seminary in New York. While there he was involved in the work of the Abyssinian Baptist Church in Harlem, an experience that confirmed his opposition to racist social policy, especially as it applied to the Jewish issue. In North America his cultural experience was further augmented with vacation visits to Cuba and Mexico.

Back in Berlin as a lecturer in the University, Bonhoeffer made clear his opposition to the Nazi Party even before it came to power in 1933. His sharpest opposition was expressed in reaction to Reichsbischof Müller and his role in leadership of the German Christians who were bent on directing the church as an agency of the state. As a member of the Confessing Church, Bonhoeffer vigorously opposed the Aryan clause that had been imposed on the national Church with terms that forbade appointment of Jews to serve in church offices or to receive ordination qualifying for parish ministry. Together with Martin Niemoller and others, he was a founder of the Pastors' Emergency League to help clergy cope with the rising Nazi intimidation of the churches.

During the years 1933–35 Bonhoeffer was commissioned to minister in two expatriate German churches in London. There he greatly enhanced his ecumenical contacts, especially with George Bell, Bishop of Chichester, with whom he was to have a clandestine relationship during the war years when they shared information relating to the German Resistance. During his London ministry, Bonhoeffer enjoyed association with the Mirfield Fathers and the Community of the Resurrection. From them he developed sympathy with the monastic experience that could be seen reflected in the course of studies he developed for the Confessing Church students he taught during 1935–37 at Finkenwalde. In light of that theological interest, Bonhoeffer's disappointment was understandable when circumstances obliged him to decline an invitation from Mahatma Gandhi to attend one of his ashrams in India. In September 1937 Bonhoeffer's seminary was closed by government order, and Bonhoeffer and colleagues were banned from teaching or living in Berlin.

For a time thereafter he continued to have limited pastoral duties in Pomerania. In early 1939 he was able to travel to England to visit his twin sister who, for security, had moved there with her Jewish husband. While in London, he met ecumenical friends including Bishop Bell, Willem Visser 't Hooft and Reinhold Niebuhr. Having no definite assignment in Germany, he accepted an invitation from Niebuhr to assume a year's teaching assignment at Union Theological Seminary in New York. In the end, it was to be a very brief interlude of little more than a month. As war became ever more imminent, Bonhoeffer in New York underwent struggles of conscience and decided that he must go back to share the fate of family and associates in the Confessing Church. He reached England on 27 July 1939 on the last crossing of the Bremen.

As a convinced pacifist, his immediate concern was to avoid a draft into the Nazi military forces. His offer to serve in the army chaplaincy was refused. At that point he decided to accept an offer from his brother-in-law Hans von Dohnányi to serve under his command as a member of the Abwehr. This was a largely civilian secret service that gathered wide-ranging information of interest to the army. Four Bonhoeffer family members became major participants in this unit; besides Hans and Dietrich, brother Klaus and a second brother-in-law, Rüdiger Schleicher, were involved under the general command of Admiral Canaris. In consequence of that involvement, all five were ultimately executed in April 1945 as conspirators against the life of Hitler.

A conspiratorial group had for years existed within the Abwehr. Records showed that they were at the point of assassinating Hitler during the Czechoslovakian crisis in 1938. The plan fell through when Hitler withheld attack – disappointed, it was believed, that the British and French prime ministers were not intimidated by his threats against the Czechs but agreed to sign the Munich Agreement.

Under the Abwehr cover, Bonhoeffer had considerable freedom to travel and make churchly contacts during 1940–43 with visits in Scandinavian countries, in Italy, and on three occasions in Switzerland where he conferred with Visser 't Hooft on plans that anticipated the postwar founding of the World Council of Churches. At a church conference in Sweden he conferred with Bishop Bell, who was conveying messages from the British Government. With these activities Bonhoeffer coped with issues of Christian conscience and national loyalty, being convinced that only the death of Hitler could bring closure to his evil regime.

In January 1943 he became engaged to Maria von Wedemeyer, a brilliant young woman half his age. Years later the partial publication of their correspondence added significant perspectives on events in the period. In 1943, however, the impending threat to Bonhoeffer's freedom and survival loomed large when two attempts on the life of Hitler failed during March, thereby stirring a major investigation. One immediate result was Bonhoeffer's arrest on 5 April 1943 and his incarceration in Tegel military prison in Berlin to await interrogation and trial.

The same event led to the beginning of his fruitful

exchange of letters with his dialogue partner, Eberhard Bethge, an opportunity facilitated by sympathetic prison wardens. Bonhoeffer carried on with writing, aided by books sent by his family and supported by twice monthly visits permitted to his fiancée. A striking change in theological outlook emerged in his letter of 10 April 1944 to Bethge in which he intimated his proposal for a transition to *religionless Christianity*. Letters in this vein continued for five months until failure of a last bold assassination attempt on 20 July 1944 engineered by Lieutenant Colonel von Stauffenberg. Shortly thereafter Bonhoeffer was placed in the Gestapo prison in Berlin and communication gradually ended as he was moved successively to Buchenwald, then Regensburg, and finally to Flossenburg camp in Bavaria, where he was summarily tried and executed by hanging on 9 April 1945. It is believed that he continued to work on a manuscript until his last day, but no record of it remains.

Bonhoeffer's critique of religion did not extend to the point of dismissing all the history and phenomena of world religions. What he sought to dismiss was the *religious a priori*; that is, he wanted to remove the tendency, common in the Christian sphere, of addressing every problem in the natural realm by first seeking a religious solution, as if science and common wisdom were not available. He believed that the record of historical experience would show that in many cases the religious and non-religious solutions to problems were identical. In that case, scientific solutions were likely to be both obvious and superior.

Bonhoeffer's most striking expression for guiding the future of Christian thought was his insistence that we must regard the world as having come-of-age (*mundige Welt*) in the modern era of scientific and social learning and control. In practice, science does not turn to religion to solve its problems. On the other hand we see people of traditional religious values resorting to a deus ex machina solution of problems and questions. When solutions do emerge they are often accepted as achievements effected through divine power. Bonhoeffer mused that for 1900 years the faith had been enclosed in a religious garment that amounted to a metaphysical system, though one lacking philosophical criticism. Too often the embrace of religion has led to creation of a sphere of holiness that we ourselves have identified and sanctified. Bonhoeffer felt that the problem of shedding religiosity in our time was comparable to the struggle of the early church to be free of the Jewish requirement of circumcision.

In implied criticism of the Lutheran emphasis on salvation by faith alone, he turned to emphasizing ethical action. His volume *Ethics* contains many of the insights that survived from fragments of text that were spirited out of prison and represented what he hoped would become his major work.[2] Central to his

---

2. Dietrich Bonhoeffer, *Ethics,* ed. Eberhard Bethge (London: SCM Press, 1955).

ethical views was his criticism of the religiosity that often substitutes for moral action. He insisted that "it is not the religious act that makes the Christian but participation in the sufferings of God in the secular life."[3]

He maintained that the real transcendence does not reside in the beyond but in the person next to you. To live according to the pattern of Jesus, as the man for others, is to relate to true transcendence. We have to live in the world as though God does not exist. It is in his weakness he saves us. "God allows himself to be edged out of the world and on to the cross. God is weak and powerless in the world, and that is exactly the way, the only way, in which he can be with us and help us."[4]

In keeping with this assertion Bonhoeffer held that it is foolish and presumptuous for us to be constantly gathering our powers to save the church. He wanted Christians to speak of God, not just in times of distress, or in fear of death at the edges of life, but at the centre of life and goodness. Speaking out of this perspective Bonhoeffer made the admission that increasingly he found it easier to talk about religion with secular people. Discussing religion with religious people became strained because they were concerned with retaining the proper sanctity and religious protocols. In view of this observation he found that he was

---

3. Dietrich Bonhoeffer, *Letters and Papers from Prison,* ed. Eberhard Bethge (London: SCM Press, 1953), 18 July 1944.
4. Ibid., 16 July 1944.

gaining more satisfaction from reading the Old Testament because it avoided direct address of the divine name. In consequence, its language is otherwise direct and concrete in every context. For Bonhoeffer, the new way of speaking of God was by recognizing God in human form, in the neighbour within reach. The way of being Christian is thus twofold: engaging in prayer and social action.

Although lacking the final definitive structure that Bonhoeffer had in mind before his voice was stilled, his biographers have sketched a vague outline of what they believe the book might have offered:

Chapter 1. Taking stock of Christianity in a world come-of-age. No longer needing God as a stopgap.

Chapter 2. What really is Christian faith? Who is God? Being there for others, the real transcendence.

Chapter 3. The church is the church only when it is there for others. It must be faced toward the world.

Included in Bonhoeffer's literary legacy are several poems conveying the profundity of thought and feeling that upheld him through lonely hours of imprisonment. Exemplary was the poem *Stations on the Way to Freedom*. The fourth station is Death. These lines may have been on his mind as he walked to the gallows announcing to a companion, "This is the end, for me the beginning of life":

> *Come now, highest of feasts on the way to freedom eternal,*
> *Death, strike off the fetters, break down the walls that oppress us,*
> *Our bedazzled soul and our ephemeral body,*
> *That we may see at last the sight that here was not vouchsafed us.*
> *Freedom, we sought you long in discipline, action, suffering.*
> *Now as we die we see you and know you at last, face to face.*[5]

In summary review of Bonhoeffer's place in twentieth-century theology, we have to begin with the weight of political factors affecting his esteem. The early British estimate of his importance was a reflection of the ecumenical contacts he had developed in Western Europe and the United States. In the first postwar weeks when Bonhoeffer became known through Bethge's *Letters and Papers from Prison*, the non-German readers were disposed to savour the fact that he had been a significant opponent of Hitler and his regime. In Germany, on the other hand, there remained a considerable weight of opinion that regarded him as a traitor to his nation. A recent appreciative biography in German noted that by the end of the century, and with major historical reviews of secret records showing Bonhoeffer's courageous commitment to a Chris-

---

5. Bonhoeffer, *Ethics*, xv.

tian social order, his name and martyrdom have assumed an honoured place in his own country.[6]

During a week in midsummer of 1945, while the British public was overcoming the shock of seeing pictures of liberated concentration camps, friends of Bonhoeffer, including Bishop Bell, organized a memorial service to Bonhoeffer in Holy Trinity Church in Kingsway, London, which was broadcast by the BBC and heard in Germany. In due course a statue of Bonhoeffer was sculpted on a wall of Westminster Abbey to stand alongside those of other twentieth-century Christian martyrs.

The Bonhoeffer heritage hardly inspired a school of disciples, but it did evoke interest that forced a radical shift among postwar thinkers who wanted to expand further upon the non-religious ideas and rhetoric suggested by his latest reflections. Books appeared, such as *The Secular City* by Harvey Cox, *The Secular Meaning of the Gospel* by Paul van Buren and *The Gospel of Christian Atheism* by Thomas Altizer. Bishop John Robinson's widely read and debated book, *Honest to God*, introduced elements of Bonhoeffer's thought to a literate public. Traces of the same radical modality later appeared in the God is Dead movement, which sounded an echo of Nietzsche's confession of deicide at the dawn of the twentieth century.

In any discussion of these literatures, it is difficult to make meaningful commentary that does not

---

6. Schlingensiepen, *Dietrich Bonhoeffer 1906–45*, xv–xvi; 406, note 3.

employ the language, literature, and historic institutional and cultural features of religion. It would not seem amiss to take note of the fact that on the second to last day of his life Dietrich Bonhoeffer deferred to traditional sentiments of established religion. After conducting worship with one roomful of prisoners in the school building at Flossenburg, he at first declined a request to do the same with a second group, noting that they were mainly Catholics plus one Russian atheist. When he was assured that they would not suffer any liturgical discomfort, he responded positively and conducted his final worship service, using the religious Offices for the Day.

Interpretation of Texts

THE GOD HERMES WAS RECOGNIZED as speaker on behalf of all other deities in the classic pantheon. The search for singular clarity in verbal expression has fittingly appropriated the title of the ancient god to identify the discipline of hermeneutics.

Interpretation theory in modern practice has been associated with the meaning of texts stemming from the long history of translating and exegeting ancient scriptures. The Protestant tradition in particular has borne much of this undertaking for the Christian scriptures.

In broader perspective, however, hermeneutical principles are in play in critical interpretation pertaining to rhetoric, art, jurisprudence, historical records and a wide range of sociocultural practice. In the natural sciences similar discernment is called for in paleontology, anthropology, and kindred archaeological studies.

Hermeneutics in the twentieth century made a significant advance through the groundbreaking researches of Schleiermacher in the previous century.

Where earlier study of texts had focused on discerning the mind and intention of the author, his interpretation considered how it affected the mind of the reader. He valued the text for the extent to which it promoted the self-understanding of the reader. That approach embraced also an understanding of psychology and other studies of human behaviour viewed scientifically.

A weakness in his undertaking lay in the fact that he was striving to achieve a universal hermeneutical methodology that lacked a sufficient account of the unique features occurring in literary form and in the distinctive culture of the individual reader. It was nevertheless a marked advance from traditional Bible study methods that are still practised in conservative circles, which is asking the Bible to interpret itself, wresting proof texts from it and favouring the use of reference editions of the Bible for guidance through its contents.

Hermeneutics in the latter half of the twentieth century largely featured more recent German scholarship and the widespread debates that it encouraged, beginning with the work of Rudolph Bultmann.

BULTMANN

The dramatic proposal from famed New Testament scholar Rudolph Bultmann (1884–1976) for a radical demythologizing of the New Testament created surprise in the academic community for two main reasons. He had been formerly associated with Barth in the early days of the Crisis Theology and had remained supportive of the Confessing Church. Further cause for surprise was the dating of the key essay that opened the demythologizing controversy. The essay was published in 1941 at the height of World War II, when demands on parish leadership and state security should have been occupying the minds of those given to scholarly pursuits. It was more than a decade later before the English-speaking world joined in the debate following the publication of Ian Smith's book *Myth in the New Testament*.[1]

In his essay Bultmann sought to clarify the meaning of myth and how it might assist in understanding the authentic self. He stated that the real purpose of myth is not to aid understanding of the world as it is, but to express our understanding of ourselves in the world in which we live. Myths should be expressed not cosmologically but anthropologically or (better still) existentially.

Bultmann did not spare the sensibilities of conservative readers. He spelled out the mythological patterns of New Testament cosmology and story telling. He questioned how twentieth-century persons of normal education could take seriously the description of a three-decker universe, a six-day creation of the planet Earth, or the ending of the same with an apocalyptic

---

1. Ian Smith, *Myth in the New Testament* (London: SCM Press, 1952).

parousia. He did not believe that modern people could accept the idea of virgin birth, the assumption that illness is caused by demonic beings, or that death is a punishment for sin. He directly reminded his readers that the Bible must be read through a scientific lens.[2]

Bultmann did not mean to disillusion his readers. Like preachers of other times he tried to bridge the gap between the first and later centuries. His demythologizing was intended to make the *kerygma* comprehensible to his contemporaries in order that they might be brought to faith – and he was a persuasive person. Bultmann's preaching and teaching had a strong impact on his students. I heard late-night passionate debates raging between many of his former students who had migrated from Marburg to Basel and were encountering neo-orthodox disciples of Barth.

Two German terms were prominent in Bultmann's discourse: *Historia* and *Geschichte.* The first term signifies scientifically verified reporting and evaluating of historical speech or events. The second term also signifies the historical, but it conveys the added meaning of embracing and appropriating the significance of the history portrayed. The meaning may have a life beyond the place and time of the remembered speech or event. This use of language bore a historical link with the seminal thought of Martin Kähler whose influence had extended also to Barth. The title of Kähler's principal nineteenth-century publication suggests a

---

2. Hans-Werner Bartsch, ed., *Kerygma and Myth: a Theological Debate* (London: SPCK, 1953), 10.

critical distinction between the history depicting the life and teaching of Jesus and the decision of faith that responds believingly to Christ as Messiah.[3]

The development of Bultmann's theology reflected at many points his early colleagueship at Marburg with existentialist philosopher Martin Heidegger, who became something of a philosophical mentor. Such a role has clear theological precedents, recalling the early Church Fathers with their strong Platonist references, and the Aristotelian structure in Aquinas' *Summa Theologica*. For Bultmann, Heidegger's search for temporal self-understanding resonated with the Christian view of living toward the end, eschatologically. Heidegger regarded the authentic life as one lived with care toward death, overcoming the fallenness we experience as human subjects who are simply thrust into the world. We exist with an awareness of a transcendent relation through which we hear the mysterious *call of conscience,* a call from the beyond to the beyond.

For Heidegger, however, there was no objective transcendent. The search for authenticity was to be understood as our attempt to overcome casualness or everydayness in our living. Being authentic requires deliberate resolve. For Bultmann the authentic life is a passing from the old life of moral degeneracy to a new one enabled by a work of grace.[4] The redemptive grace

---

3. Martin Kähler, *The Historical Jesus and the Historical Biblical Christ* (Philadelphia: Fortress Press, 1964).
4. John Macquarrie, *An Existentialist Theology* (London: SCM Press, 1955).

is conveyed in the *kerygma,* affirming the message of the Cross and Resurrection of Jesus. The transforming role of Jesus is not to be contemplated in detached objectivity as though it were an ordinary event in human evolution and history. The cross is *geschichtlich,* an event of cosmic proportions that brings judgment to the world. Concerning Jesus there are historic facts that must be accepted – above all the fact that the apostles saw and believed the events of Cross and Resurrection. Our conviction regarding these events is established through hearing the preached word. Speaking of Jesus he says, "He meets us in the word of preaching and nowhere else. The faith of Easter is just this – faith in the word of preaching."[5] The claim is a distant echo of a line from Kähler in the previous century: "The real Christ is the Christ who is preached."[6] The immediacy proclaimed suggests that the response of faith to the *kerygma* is an existential experience not translatable into everyday terms. This insistence upon revelatory uniqueness meant that Bultmann did not follow Heidegger after the latter's turn to linguisticality.[7]

---

5. Bartsch, ed., *Kerygma and Myth,* 41.

6. Ibid., 66.

7. Heidegger, however, made an important linguistic point in his perception of the modalities of speaking and hearing, of silence and waiting. The point is worthy of emphasis when we consider how often the language of religious devotion is expressed under the weight of practised mantras.

GADAMER

Hans-Georg Gadamer was arguably the pre-eminent hermeneutical philosopher of the twentieth century. After having made his major scholarly contribution, in retirement he travelled widely and engaged in dialogue with numerous contemporaries. In so doing, he was also demonstrating the dialogical or conversational character of his approach to interpretation of ideas in texts. He made no attempt at conclusive rational objectivity in discerning the meaning of texts; rather, he sought to discover meaning as it emerged in intersubjective communication. In his major work he depicts what we actually do as we interpret text, rather than establishing some general goal for hermeneutical inquiry.[8]

As Heidegger's student (and later his colleague), Gadamer begins with the process of interpreting based on self-understanding. He reminds us that our understanding of a text or situation is always based on the foundation of prior involvement. We begin on the basis of our history, our effectual historical consciousness as he describes it. The historically grounded self-awareness constitutes our personal horizon, the self with which we encounter and engage the horizon of another person or set of ideas alien to us. When the meeting between our own self-understanding and the horizon of the other subject leads to agreement, we are thereby experiencing a fusion of horizons. The

---

8. Gadamer, *Truth and Method*.

outcome of this fusion is an incremental disclosure of meaning; as a result, therefore, we move forward with an augmented effective historical consciousness.

Following Heidegger's metaphor of the hermeneutical circle, Gadamer regarded traversing the circle as an ongoing process rather than as a symbol of perfection or completion. The provisional advance in understanding spurs us to consider continuing enquiry, but we must accept the fact that self-understanding is never complete. As Anthony Thistleton expressed it, "hermeneutics ... begins with the recognition that historical conditionedness is two-sided. The modern interpreter no less than the text stands in a given historical context and tradition."[9]

This calls for analyzing the two horizons of author and reader, just as in conversations there is an interchange of mutually shared themes or interests. The metaphor of the horizon suggests that there is always more back of the horizon than is immediately disclosed when it presents as a basis for fusion. We are challenged to come to a fuller understanding of the alien horizon in its linguistic and cultural features. The greater challenge may be to discern the features of our personal horizon, being aware that self-knowledge is never complete. If we claim completeness, we are presuming to complete the circle, the symbol of perfection. The symbol of the circle in the sense applied by Heidegger is a dynamic spiral sphere, with each

---

9. Anthony Thistleton, *The Two Horizons* (Grand Rapids: Eerdmans, 1980), 11.

revolution falling short of ideality in historical time. Tradition thereby is developed further and enriched, as the process continually unfolds.

Without in any way dismissing the circle as the symbol of incremental advancement of understanding, I have argued that the arc can be a supplementary symbol for the uncovering of meaning in regional and limited issues where the fusing of horizons on a full scale might distort the exercise of judgment or where a sharper focus is indicated. The arc is the only geometric figure that could connect the opposing horizons in a single field of vision.[10]

The arc figure suggests that the horizons of text and interpreter may need a little space and time between them before attempting to make their fusion complete. The perspectives of text and interpreter may need to be held for a time in binocular focus, recognizing both their connectedness and their distance.

The place for binocular vision may be illustrated from the history of Christian theology. The first major melding of biblical text and cultural awareness occurred when the Greco-Roman world came into intellectual embrace with leading Christian theologians during the first four centuries of the Christian era. This was history that modern ecumenical moves have recapitulated to a marked degree. The Protestant emphasis on *sola scriptura* meant that textual studies

---

10. Paul Ricœur, *Hermeneutics and the Human Sciences* (Cambridge, MA: Cambridge University Press, 1981); James Farris, "The Hermeneutical Arc," *Toronto Journal of Theology* 4, no. 1 (1988): 86.

had to wait two centuries for the scientific interpretation of text and history to produce what we now recognize as modern biblical scholarship. The metaphor of the arc encourages the holding of tentative understanding while awaiting fuller disclosure and insight.

Gadamer's major advance in hermeneutics was his critique of the Cartesian post-Enlightenment dismissal of prejudice. Prejudice so understood called for the subjectivity of the researcher or historical observer to be removed from the equation to allow scientific measure and conclusions to have unqualified play. Mathematics became the norm of disinterested objectivity, the ideal of pure research.

Gadamer countered with the claim that truth-seeking leads us beyond methodology to engage in philosophy. Philosophically the quest of understanding requires us to do preliminary selecting and shaping of questions for making discovery. We have to recognize that self-knowledge must ever be refined until we accept the fact that "self-understanding can no longer be integrally related to a complete self-transparency. The sense of a full presence of ourselves to ourselves, namely self-understanding, is always on the way; it is on a path whose completion is a clear impossibility." What the real self may yet become looms only in the subconscious.[11]

The realization that we have only limited self-awareness alongside the imponderables and alien

---

11. Hans-Georg Gadamer, *Reason in the Age of Science* (Cambridge: MIT Press, 1981), 103.

features of the other encountered horizon is a constant emphasis in the work of Paul Ricœur. On his terms, the whole hermeneutic enterprise responds to a suspicion that risk is always present in making an interpretation. But the real risk may reside in ideological features in ourselves that we have not fully analyzed. Psychoanalysis and the critique of ideology are therefore studies that may help us frame the questions that we wish to resolve.

The translating of text from one language to another is the most transparent case of hermeneutics viewed as an art. The more adequate translation is the one where the translator moves alien text into her/his mother tongue. The challenge is to become at home in the foreign tongue in its historical and cultural environment. This goes far beyond settling on lexical equivalence. The translator's role is thus an historical one. Both the work of the original author and that of the translation may over time take on an element of classicism. When either or both works are submitted to the world, it may be found that the author wrote this piece beyond his/her original intention or capability. Time and cultural change may cause the text to yield more, or different, significance than was foreseen or intended. The greater challenge may apply to the text that is already a translation, for example a Greek and Latin translation into English, with a global language outstripping the historical origins of such a text.

Gadamer's reflection on the origin of a work of art draws attention to the surplus of meaning that may reside in a work while awaiting the play of hermeneutical imagination. The work continues over time to stir the artistic sensibilities of its public. An obscure Grecian urn inspired John Keats to draw imaginative pictures to populate a world unperceived by the initial artist. The work of art does not have a past, but it has an unfolding contemporaneity that awaits aesthetic stimulation and creativity. Likewise the reproductive arts represented by music and theatre reflect the growth in meaning realized through repeated performances of the work and the extent to which these also reveal interpretive insights. Advancements in technical media may also intervene, confirming the validity in Marshall McLuhan's aphorism that "the medium is the message."

In Gadamer's view the guiding principle of communication is belief that the disclosure of meaning is the disclosure of a world. And in that disclosure the *application* must be a governing concern. Gadamer stands by the principle that "application is neither a subsequent nor merely occasional part of the phenomenon of understanding, but it codetermines it from the beginning."[12]

In considering the application of interpretation the key term is *practice*. The validity and usefulness of the interpretation is made evident in its power to inform practice. A case in point would be the long tradition of identifying the vocations of law and medicine as *practices*. The tradition would appear to stem from

---

12. Gadamer, *Truth and Method*, 289.

the fact that these two professions involve diagnostic and legal determinations that are kindred to hermeneutical discovery. Gadamer's contribution would appear to be eminently more suited to mentoring the legal profession. He stresses that "the legal historian cannot simply take the original application of the law as determining its original meaning. As an historian he will have to take account of the historical changes that the law has undergone." Individual laws become valid through being interpreted and applied.[13]

In conversation with Jürgen Habermas and Paul Ricœur on communicative action, Gadamer demonstrated his agreement with the view that the hermeneutics of action is a pervasive issue for study and debate among social scientists. It was clear, however, that Gadamer did not fully share Habermas' neo-Marxist and materialistic views of history. His own position relied heavily on philosophical review and ethical application. He believed that all historical understanding is founded on a work of hermeneutics and the application of meanings discovered. He did not believe that wholeness of understanding justified a doctrine of universal history as in Hegelian idealism. Understanding effective history requires extended and patient review and the fusing of horizons to promote understanding. A provisional vision of the whole is essential to the task but it awaits delimitation. The process of interpreting communicative action is sure-

---

13. Paul Ricœur, *Hermeneutics and the Human Sciences* (Cambridge: Cambridge University Press, 1981), 290.

ly the end sought in the work of the historian. In theological terms interpretation has to be pursued under guidance of a moral and spiritual compass.

Gadamer's contribution to hermeneutical theory and practice was distinguished by the place he awarded to history. It informed the two major themes that functioned in his teaching: effective historical consciousness, and the horizons of sameness and difference that combine to yield a world. In briefer summary, his views on the philosophy of history could be effectively expressed in terms of Hegel's aphorism: "The history of the world is the judgment of the world" (*Weltgeschichte ist Weltgericht*).

Interpreting Stories: Theirs and Ours

To this point, my discussion of the heritage of philosophical and theological reflection has been largely textual. Many of the same elements of criticism are involved when examining the historical judgment of moral issues that may have far-reaching practical effect. Other evaluations are required in proximity to the action itself, such as the aesthetic evaluation of liturgical expression or of art and music.

Profound religious traditions underlie the production of many ancient monuments that invite spiritual devotion. The stone placements of Stonehenge and the Egyptian pyramids are cases in point. Archaeological digs continue to convey cultural and political records of civilizations long extinct. The discovery and preservation of the Dead Sea Scrolls has aided greatly in reviewing the biblical literary heritage and cultural circumstances of the Jewish people leading up to the Roman conquest. From archival digs we are able to reconstruct the history and fortunes of peoples long forgotten as a result of natural disasters, and sometimes through decline in the will to survive felt by a people whose gods have failed. Occasionally in our times we may observe anthropological and archaeological interest appearing at a very mundane level in terms of community projects to explore the *sociology of garbage.*

A marked advance in our ability to understand other times and people appeared with the turn to relational modes of thought. Kierkegaard and a coterie of existentialist writers promoted this turning away from the rigorous subject/object template of post-Enlightenment thought. It has encouraged engagement with themes of transcendence, perhaps even in relation to the person next to us, to use Bonhoeffer's phrase. The immediacy of relation is illustrated in the bond between a speaker and a hearer or reader. The story form is an important mode of interpretive communication because it normally includes a plot with development moving to a conclusion. For this reason, the story is often a meaningful and engaging means of communicating political, social, and religious themes. The power of the Bible to convey its message has really been the stories that it projects despite any problems of translation and cultural disconnection.

When we attempt to tell stories and to understand those that others tell us, it is important to overcome both narcissism and the self-absorbed attitudes of assumed exceptionalism. As Paul Ricœur has reminded us, we need to learn to regard our self as the other.[1] For a social entity it is likewise essential that its collective membership should see itself objectively as other in relation to the societies it may encounter. Fortunately some stories with moral import are foisted upon the public consciousness in ways that force us to see ourselves as others see us, and to recognize how popular and comfortable social customs or benefits may have blinded us from seeing our complicity in wrongdoing.

For many decades in the twentieth century South African governments imposed the racist policy of apartheid on the majority of their citizens, while presenting themselves self-righteously as representative orthodox Christians. When the story of Nelson Mandela's "long walk to freedom" became a world news drama, it was not long before political and social integration followed. The subsequent Truth and Reconciliation Commission exercise has yielded remarkable stories of harm and healing in an attempt to write a new story. (A comparable story of injustice visited on aboriginal children of Canada through the former residential schools program is being heard in Canada, with only provisional resolution to date.)

In the United States the convulsive struggle to overcome the heritage of slavery and racial segregation waited for stories that included *Uncle Tom's Cabin*, the account of Rosa Parks' bus ride, and the "I have a dream" speech from the Lincoln Memorial to precipi-

---

[1]. Paul Ricœur, *One's Self as an Other* (Chicago: University of Chicago Press, 1995).

tate the legislative and social revolution that promised an end to racial injustice. (A remarkable result of that last story has been the erection of a statue honouring Martin Luther King, Jr. on the Washington Mall.)

Familiarity with stories having moral or spiritual import can have the effect of leaving us seeming insensitive to the *message*. This has been an admission by many readers of the New Testament prompted by the Liberation Theology movement to discover in the teaching of Jesus a radical social gospel proclaiming a preferential option for the poor. A powerful spokesman from Latin America for this reading was Gustavo Gutiérrez, who blamed historical prejudice for the long delay in both spiritual liberation and its civil counterpart. He was convinced that a skewing of history occurred because most historical narratives have been written by the winners in the contests of life, rather than by the losers. He pointed out "human history is written by a white hand, a male hand from the dominating social class. The perspective of the defeated in history is different." They are able to discover that "where hunger is, God is not."[2]

Feminists too are convinced that their stories have been similarly repressed in church and society. Elisabeth Schüssler Fiorenza has demonstrated that the story of women involved in Christian origins has to be uncovered by an extraordinary effort in historical research. She maintains that women's exclusion from their own history has been responsible for their loss of

---

2. Gustavo Gutiérrez, *The Witness* (April 1976), 6.

power in the church. In recovering that hidden history, she insists "it is necessary to go beyond the limits of the New Testament canon since it is a product of the patristic church, that is, a theological document of the historical winners." From her research, she concludes that "women as church have a continuous history and tradition that can claim Jesus and the prism of the earliest church as its biblical route, mode or prototype, one that is open to feminist transformation."[3]

In general comment on the interpretive review of religious text and context, it must be stressed that this is a continuing task for theologians. Because interpretation is pre-eminently an historical undertaking, we who interpret history are constantly subject to pejorative criticism deriding us as *revisionists*. Admittedly, there is always a risk of crossing the line from review to authorial invention.

Interpreted action, rather than text, however, is more likely to be based on unique happenings. In fact, their renewed uplifting and repeated hearing as words and events is the only reliable historical approach to their interpretation we can have. Paul Ricœur has insisted that historical views are not conclusions, but resolutions in process of further refinement by succeeding generations of scholars. The assumption that we can go behind temporal experience and viewpoints to a pristine encounter with the past has humorously

---

3. Elisabeth Schüssler Fiorenza, *In Memory of Her, a Feminist Theological Reconstruction of Christian Origins* (New York: Crossroads, 1994), xv.

been likened to a moralizing attempt to restore virginity. Historical narrative must proceed rather with the realization that we are making entries in an ongoing story that will be expanded and edited by successive generations.

INTERPRETING RELIGIONS: TRADITION AND DIALOGUE

Study of the history and phenomenology of religion has not generally been given a central place in Western theology. The eclipse of Greek and Roman religion and the mystery cults at the dawn of the Christian era led to religion being identified as Judeo-Christian in large areas of the Mediterranean basin. In light of this the student of religions other than Christianity must be mindful of religious attitudes that need correction through wide reading of unfamiliar religious texts.

In the case of Islam, which emerged after the early period of Christian dominance, its sameness and difference presents a special issue for balanced understanding. While Islam succeeded in gaining dominance over the domain of Judeo-Christianity in the Mediterranean region and survived the failed effort of the Crusades to dislodge it, the Holy Roman Empire regained its power even after the loss of the Byzantine empire in the East. The Church maintained its strong foothold supported by the vigorous move on the part of Christian states to advance their position by geographic explorations and colonial development. It was in Christian lands that the post-Enlightenment development of science and technology sparked political and cultural dominance. The development of printing, coinciding with the Protestant Reformation, gave supervening literary advantage to Christian Europe. Despite these advantages the scholarly study of religion as a feature of life open to detailed examination received little attention prior to the nineteenth century. Until that time the principal source materials had been reports from missionary experiences, combined with occasional travellers' tales.

A more serious level of enquiry emerged with the psychological descriptions of Schleiermacher in which he identified religion as consisting of the feeling of absolute dependence. This approach from the perspective of the social sciences was soon followed by varied sociological and historical reviews. A broad-ranging scholarly descriptive account of the variety and venues associated with world religious development had to wait upon a series of studies by the anthropologist James Fraser, completed in 1915.[4] In theological focus, a major study of the phenomena of religion appeared in the 1917 publication of Rudolf Otto's *Das Heilige*.[5] Despite the timing – during a period of unholy slaughter involving the great world powers – it became one of the most widely read books

---

4. *The Golden Bough*.
5. First published in English translation by Oxford University Press in 1923. Rudolf Otto, *The Idea of the Holy*, trans. J. W. Harvey (New York: Penguin, 1959).

of the twentieth century. Its prominence was achieved notwithstanding the effect of neo-Orthodox proscriptions against any characterizations of religion as the anthropological deifying of humanistic values. Otto, for his part, sidestepped the problem by defining religion as the numinous, a quality both terrifying and fascinating at the same time. He represented it as an irreducible and original category existing in its own terms, rather than merely as a qualifying adjective. His view of religion was to have an acknowledged effect on Paul Tillich's definition of religion as *ultimate concern,* a broad definition that could cover the spiritual experience of manifold individuals and societies. Mircea Eliade acknowledged Otto's knowledge and influential contribution to his own book[6] and to his subsequent editorship of the *Encyclopedia of Religion* in sixteen volumes.[7]

Since much of the reporting on religion has been done with comparative assumptions drawn from Christian religion, it is anomalous that official agencies in the Christian church have been very late in publically acknowledging the other faiths. The neglect can be traced until 1965 and Vatican II which brought forward its "Declaration of the Church to non-Christian Religions." The title of the Declaration itself, however, pronounced a continuing negative identification of faiths other than Christian. The one religious trad-

---

6. Mircea Eliade, *The Sacred and the Profane: The Nature of Religion* (New York: Harcourt, 1956).
7. Mircea Eliade, ed., *Encyclopedia of Religion* (New York: Macmillan, 1987).

ition, apart from Christianity, outlined with special care in the document was Judaism, a kindred faith. Belatedly in 1971 the World Council of Churches established a secretariat devoted to promoting relations with people of other faiths. This could be described as an extension of the ecumenism that had earlier developed among Protestant churches engaged in shared mission among people of other faiths.

In the aftermath of World War II the experience of many military personnel, especially Americans, led to a new interest in discovering the belief systems and phenomena of religions that had been encountered in the context of military operations. The academic response to that interest promoted a major increase in the faculties of religious studies in universities and colleges. A notable mark in this interest was the appointment of the historian Arnold Toynbee to deliver the famed Gifford Lectures on religion at Edinburgh in 1952–53.[8]

Through the historian's lens, Toynbee made his judgments about the great religions viewed within a time frame of 2,500 years. He concluded that eight major religious traditions have arisen and maintained continuity within that period. They are identified as philosophical Confucianism and Theravada Buddhism, the longest enduring; they were followed by Zoroastrianism, Judaism, Christianity, Hinduism, Mahayana Buddhism, and Islam.

---

8. Arnold Toynbee, *An Historian's Approach to Religion* (London: Oxford University Press, 1956).

This conspectus included the decisive time which Karl Jaspers identified as the axial period, occurring about 800–820 BCE, when great leaders emerged, including Confucius, Buddha, Lao-tzu, the classical Greek philosophers, and the great prophets of Israel. All of these exerted great political and cultural influence as well as religious. From his review, Toynbee concluded that all eight surviving faiths have shown considerable staying power and on this reckoning will continue to exist. If they do continue to exist side by side, this militates against any singular claim to uniqueness and finality.[9]

The longevity of a religious tradition is not the measure of its importance. Those of us listening to Toynbee's lectures at Edinburgh were troubled by the recent history of pseudo-religions that had usurped our attention in the period leading up to and following the War. The world news current with the lectures was preoccupied with the early days of the state of Israel and the counterclaims to ancient religious authority that underlay volatile conflicts then unfolding in the Middle East. In the years since then it has been increasingly the case that questions about historic sanctions have been superseded by world historical events falling outside any doctrinal orthodoxy or cultural issues that may have been in play.

The heritage of colonialism practised by the great European states or empires has seen religious conflicts occur because colonial boundaries were too often

---

9. Ibid., 136.

drawn without regard to the ethnic and religious identities of resident population groups. In many of these territories the institution of slavery and the slave trade brought arbitrary disruption of patterns of traditional religious life, especially in northern Africa. The large migration of peoples with established religious cultures has often occurred in the modern era in response to compelling economic and political conditions rather than representing a voluntary movement of people searching for more benign and promising circumstances. A case in point was the large movement of contract labourers to serve in the sugar plantations of Fiji, Mauritius, and Caribbean countries after emancipation was proclaimed in the British Empire in 1834. The subsequent artificial blending of cultures in these territories has led to continuing crises of understanding and accommodation.

An important feature affecting migration today is the fact that most migrants are leaving states where religion is on the increase and thus in sharp contrast with belief and practice within the receiving society, where religion may be largely in decline. North American Christians (for example) are increasingly interacting at some level with large immigrant populations, especially those of Middle East and Southeast Asian origin. Their numbers warrant recognition of prominent religious features. The outline sketches that follow are not more than a gesture toward satisfying that objective. It is important, however, while reflecting on general features of religion, to be reminded of the particularity of some living religions, and to honour the faith commitment of their devotees. The following representative outlines relate to religions that involved special attention in my field experience and teaching program.

JUDAISM

Christians have an intimate shared heritage with Jews based on the Hebrew Scriptures included in our Bible, and embracing familiar history and symbolism that is part of our self-understanding. The relations affecting Jews and Christians remain problematic because Christians still find it difficult to confront the anti-Semitic demons that lurk at the border of consciousness of those of us born in the first half of the twentieth century. We have memories of Jews fleeing Nazi persecution who were denied asylum, in a reprise of policies in Christian lands that for centuries excluded Jews from receiving ordinary justice and civic opportunities.

In the post-Holocaust era a troubled Christian conscience supported the Zionist aspirations. The Balfour declaration of 1917 and the Mandate following World War I favoured a rapid migration of Jews to Palestine and ultimately facilitated the unilateral declaration of Israeli statehood in 1948, in disregard of a United Nations plan for partition of Palestine. The outcome was the reclamation of a part of Palestine for a part of world Jewry. The founding of the State of Israel took place without formal declaration of the rights of the Muslim and Christian majority then resident within Palestine. In the years following, Israel has been in recurrent conflict with Arab neighbors and the Palestinians. Nominally Christian states have regularly supported the state of Israel in defiance of UN resolutions restraining Israel as the occupying power. Not all world Jews have been in support of radical Zionism, particularly those of Orthodox tradition. Many of the conservative literalist Christian right in America agree with Zionists who want the state of Israel to include all the Canaanite territory that Abraham's dream awarded to the tribes of Israel. They await an apocalyptic issue to decide the matter, one that does not recognize the partition of Palestine.

A candid historical review of Middle East politics should yield the recognition that Israel, in relation to its neighbours and world political focus, receives a vastly larger share of attention and military licence than its population and strategic geographic position would warrant. Abraham could not have foreseen issues that would engage his posterity such as balance of power or the use of weapons of ultimate terror. While tensions remain in the region, the challenge continues for a dialogue of Jews and Gentiles to support the peace of Jerusalem.

ISLAM

Christian relations with Muslims have been conflicted since the seventh century. The 1000-year dramatic expansion of Islamic territories is witness to the powerful effect of Muhammad's message in the Koran and the vigour of a movement that became multicultural and shaped by a simple creed. The Christian response was ineffective in the beginning with the failure of the military Crusades to restore the earlier Christian hegemony. At the same time, however, Muslim education, art, and architecture, developed during their high medieval culture to become models for neighbouring states. In the same period the fall of the Eastern capital of Constantinople to Turkish power in 1453 mounted a major shock to the consciousness of Christian Europe.

In Christian society fears of Muslim expansion produced an apparent state of wilful blindness among many who endured that uncomfortable passage of history. A perennial standard text in church history, authored by a Yale professor of ecclesiastical history, devoted only 6 of its 600 pages to an account of Islam, including the Crusades. No index entry referenced Islam or Mohammedanism. In contrast Muslims have not chosen to forget their former rich culture that prevailed until European colonialism and the Catholic Inquisition conspired to sideline their empire.[10]

---

10. Williston Walker, *A History of the Christian Church* (New York: Charles Scribner's Sons, 1924).

Negative sensibilities over use of the term *crusade* remain pervasive in the world of Islam. The fact that Islam within its widespread territories lacks cohesive political or religious polity accounts in large measure for the emergence of dispirited and fragmentary uprisings. These develop in face of political and cultural forces shaped largely by Christian and Western priorities. Ironically these differences arise while overlooking features of Islamic faith that parallel many aspects of the Judeo-Christian tradition. The large element of correspondence between the two Scriptures ensures some acquaintance with each other's story. Both traditions are founded on the monotheistic vision of a divine creation and a movement of history in which the judgment of history is unfolded. The individual as well as social destiny follows a developing purposive pattern. The overall religious outlook is forward-looking and missional.

Christian thought, however, has moved to adopt a critical historical and literary outlook that challenges the verbal inspirationist views in Muslim regard for the Koran. The Muslim drive to fulfill an historic destiny tends to be characterized by a masculinity that is not sensitive to Christian views of sexual equality and the advancement of social values and human rights. The encounter of the two religions today is highlighted in the extensive Muslim migration into lands of Western Europe and North America. Expansionist moves by Islam will place increasing pressure on host jurisdictions to adopt elements of Sharia law and potentially to accommodate differing views of economic practice, human rights, dress modes, and codes of family honour. Not surprisingly, some features of current disorder stem from colonial history when populations with established religious cultures were consigned to live within counter-cultural jurisdictions at the whim or convenience of the colonial masters.

HINDUISM

My academic introduction to Hinduism was an assignment to study the volume entitled *Eastern Religions and Western Thought*, authored by Sarvepalli Radhakrishnan, the second president of independent India.[11] In this and other writings, Radhakrishnan revealed a profound philosophical knowledge of the Upanishads and sacred literatures of the other great religions of the Indian subcontinent. He made wide-ranging comparative studies of the Hindu religion showing its broad range of belief, and his own major respect for the Christian religion. In comparative reviews of Eastern and Western traditions, he emphasized that Western thought produced rational structured systems with a practical issue, whereas Eastern traditions are more meditative and feature phenomenal manifestations and emotive experiences

---

11. Sarvepalli Radhakrishnan, *Eastern Religions and Western Thought* (London: Oxford University Press, 1939).

of religious faith. They are more engaged with being than with doing.

In the Hindu tradition a broad range of belief is entertained. For those with historic interest the ancient Vedic religion offers reflective and imaginative approaches.

The Upanishads attract the attention of disciplined philosophic minds. Theologically, Hinduism falls distinctly within Toynbee's claim that all the great religions have a central commitment to a transcendent being. Hindus affirm an understanding of the Christian doctrine of the Trinity. Along with devotion to myriad gods and goddesses, there is a special devotion to Vishnu, the protector and to Shiva the action god, but embracing all is the supreme being, Brahma, completing the Trimurti. Hinduism claims also an understanding of the concept of incarnation. This is identified in the manifestation of avatars or semidivine beings that appear from time to time to reinvigorate the power and virtues of Vishnu. Such a figure was Ram, pictured in the Ramayana, a favourite story that gives biographical and dramatic support to piety.

Many of these stories celebrate the migration of the Aryan tribes from the Caucasian region to the Dravidic territories of the Indus Valley. The most popular writing known to literate Hindus is the Bhagavad Gita, which dates from the second century CE. Through the persona of Krishna, it voices the central themes of the religion. It was beloved by Gandhi, who stated that it led him to a spiritual position in which he came to regard all the great religions of the world as equal with his own. Syncretistic views of this sort have enabled Hindus to move with ease from one religion to another.

Although belief systems are not especially prescribed, ways of acting are determinative of an individual's standing within Hindu religion. Action produces a deposit of moral karma, good or bad, which is determinative of the quality of reincarnate existence.

Within the tradition karma can be advanced by adherence to the code of Manu, which prescribes participation in rites of passage. It advises on bestowal of gifts to the dead and to the god, and on rules of the patriarchal society. The code defined the role of women, which in the past bound them principally to the home and to control by male family members. The endurance of poverty and observant attention to rites of devotion, serve the up building of karma and promote release from existence in order to gain a final rebirth.

Hinduism should be recognized for its intensely social character, which features numerous pilgrimages and festive celebrations. It maintains belief that the root of human misery stems from claims made in support of separate selfhood. Pursuing individualistic objectives is to live in the state of Maya or illusion. The ideal is to arrive at a state of absorption into Nirvana in which all self-centredness disappears. In countries or communities where large East Indian groups have migrated it is important to understand how community sentiment generates patterns of association. This has been particularly evident in large Southeast Asian communities in Canada. At Richmond Hill, in Toronto, a large temple compound has been dedicated to the god Ganesh. It comprises essentially three temples with colourful icons representing Vishnu and Shiva plus many lesser deities. Devotees can be observed making devotional pujas as they move from one site to another. This compound is representative of the many holy villages found in India.

The predominant religious site in India is the city of Varanasi on the sacred Ganges. While visiting there an early morning boat rental afforded me a panoramic view of temples and the variety of worshippers bathing or meditating. Many had come to await death near the burning ghats where cremation was in constant progress, leaving the ashes of the faithful to be swept into the sacred waters. The scene reflected claims made for the pacific nature and ideals of Hinduism. At that moment, however, the recall of a current news report failed to resonate with the reflection. The Indian Army, equipped with atomic weapons, was holding training exercises nearby.

BUDDHISM

The title embraces Theravada Buddhism, which prevails in Sri Lanka and Southeast Asia, and Mahayana Buddhism, which is widely dispersed in northern

Asia. Both traditions take their source and inspiration from Gautama, a reclusive monk born of nobility, and subsequently Enlightened about 600 BCE at Bhod Gaia in India. In May of 1957 major celebrations marked the origin and history of the religion. During a visit to India in 1970 I found the celebrations continuing. These involved universities in India, but the popular culture of the religion had long since migrated to the Theravada and Mahayana countries. The early surge and development of the religion that was dominant under King Asoka in India eventually disappeared under the absorptive pressures of Hinduism.

The Buddhist features that remain characteristic of Hinduism include protection of living species, notably the bovine. The Buddha never assumed a sacred title. He chose the state in which personhood ceases through the giving up of all desire while living in this world of suffering and sorrow. Religious and moral duty is discharged by believing the elements of the religion and enduring the conclusion that suffering is universal in all life, that the cause of this is desire, and that desire can be ended by following the eightfold path. The latter is a pattern of moral discipline with moderate demand.

Theravada strikes most Christians as being far removed from the usual religious creed. It rejects theism and holds to a non-self destiny for the human person. Without belief in a supreme being or the human soul, the religion is nonetheless remarkable for affirming the concept of reincarnation. The concept envisages an individual's psychological or biological inheritance passing to a succeeding generation and persevering as a characteristic across future generations.

The Mahayana tradition, in contrast with Theravada, recognizes outstanding human qualities and achievements that constitute a transcendent abiding nature. The bearer of *RE* to a high and exemplary degree may be recognized as a bodhisattva, one who has achieved Enlightenment but holds back from assuming Buddhahood in order to extend time for supporting and guiding others to that end. Eminent ones may even transcend the rank of guides to become agents of grace, which they bestow on their followers. Such a figure was Amitabha, who achieved Buddhahood in 470 CE and was named the Buddha of Immeasurable Light. He was deemed an enabler of all who trusted in him. He became a symbol of grace received from beyond the self, rather than leaving the devotee to rely upon strenuous measures of meditative discipline, as in the rigorous practice of Zen.

The favourable view of Buddhism that is frequently found in the West shows lines of historical continuity with the biblical eras of late Hebrew and early Christian teaching upholding the primacy of grace bestowed from beyond the self. The usual benign iconography representing the Buddha resonates in limited measure with testimony to the abiding grace of Christ in Christian proclamation and symbolism. On the other hand, the negative Cassandra tone of much social criticism heard in the West echoes features of early Buddhist world-denying somberness. The secularist outlook and atheistic stance of many contemporaries in the West places them in league with strains of Theravada Buddhism.

The congenial and friendly spirit encountered within the monastic community in Sri Lanka was evident also in my experience of the scholarly community there and in India, where time for discussion was freely extended to the itinerant visitor. Notable in this regard was Dr. Gunapala P. Malalasekera who had long been the chief teacher of Buddhist thought at the University of Colombo and serving as editor of a developing *Encyclopedia of Buddhism*. In an interview he happily referred to years spent as High Commissioner to Canada and as diplomatic representative at the UN. He was anxious to discuss the latest developments in Christian theology. Later, in a letter exchange I sent him some book titles; but at that interval he died quite suddenly. Subsequently I responded to an invitation to contribute to a celebratory memorial volume in his honour.[12] In this I was able to relate to an observed interest among Buddhists in the development of European existentialism. That interest seemed fitting for a religion that concentrates more upon states of being than upon discursive argument.

In summary comment on world religions, it can be

---

12. W. J. S. Farris, "Heidegger on Language: a Path for Religious Dialogue," in *Malalasekera Commemoration Volume*, ed. O.H. de A. Wijesekera (Malalasekera Commemoration Volume Editorial Committee: Colombo, 1976), reproduced in appendix to the present volume.

confidently assumed that earlier neglect in studying religions alien to one's own will largely be overcome. Increasingly this will be a concern of politicians and journalists, if not of theologians. Countries with large populations practising religions other than Christianity are becoming ever more populous. They are also becoming more proactive politically and economically. It is a reasonable assessment that this advance will continue. Europeans and North Americans who presently know little, and probably care less, about their own religious traditions will need to become more conversant with religious calendars and their affect on agendas of political persons and regimes elsewhere.

At the same time, people who may still regard Western culture as eminently Christian are becoming aware that the sphere of religious expansion and fervour has shifted to countries of the South. This has been a development registered in the supporting membership and focus of the World Council of Churches. A similar shift in presence and influence has overtaken the Vatican. A kindred movement in world culture has unfolded more positively as the afterglow of a storied Christian mission of earlier times. Reports of the lively revival and recognition of Christian churches in China contain a story that awaits understanding and further issue.

From Cosmos to Quanta

R ELIGIOUS CULTURE IN THE WEST CANnot overlook the cosmological myths that dominate in archaic founding consciousness. Egyptian, Babylonian and Hebraic cultures shared some elements of dimly perceived origins. Sacred imagination and memory has prompted humans in general to view their lives within a framework that offers coherence to the fragmented experiences they encounter. In times past, the diurnal movement of the sun and stars and the recurring seasons may have given assurance of continuity and survival. When natural disasters and mortal plagues interfered with the pattern, there were shamanistic therapies and magical rituals dedicated to restoring harmony and thus survival. For those with a spiritual cast of mind, satisfaction may have come from some version of Shakespeare's assurance: "There's a divinity that shapes our ends / Roughhew them how we will." For considered theological interest, however, it is important to be aware of what is current in cosmology.

When we reach historical time and its scripted stories, the cosmic interest in the human condition mounts. We begin to see and foresee other times and places, and are led to speculation about movements of heavenly bodies. Astrologers develop forecasts about changes in planetary movement that are thought decisive in the destiny of individuals and societies. The French astronomer, Henri Poincaré, was led to speculate about how human insight and education would have fared, or been delayed, had Earth been covered with heavy cloud like the planet Venus. Over time, of course, differences in interpretation of cosmic phenomena have led to divided loyalties and given encouragement to the gods of war.

When the art of writing permitted self-examination at the level of social objectives, we can trace the quest for meaning and purpose as this came to be expressed in sacred scriptures. In the Hebrew scriptures, the cosmological picture is portrayed in the mythological account of Genesis. There the universe is presented as having come into being through the divine creative act. By the middle of the second century CE the archaic picture was filled out with mathematical detail in the book *Almagest,* authored by the Egyptian astronomer, Ptolemy. This account presented Earth as a flat immoveable sphere sustaining a three-decker earth formation about which the sun and other heavenly bodies circulated. The Ptolemaic version of origins persisted through the many years of theological debate and institutional development that informed the Christian Church. It remained during the flourishing period of the Islamic empire with its advanced architectural and engineering capabilities.

THE COPERNICAN REVOLUTION

After a millennium and a half of the Christian era a revolutionary shock emerged from the literally groundbreaking model of the universe presented by the Polish astronomer Copernicus in 1543. His name is commonly used to register the division between the ancient world and the post-Renaissance modern world. It was the point at which humankind was displaced from the centre of the universe. Copernicus' revolution in perspective saw the replacing of the geocentric model of the Earth with a heliocentric one, with the sun stationary amid revolving planetary bodies that included Earth. His proposal was endorsed by Galileo, augmented with his development of the telescope for distant viewing. The timeline of these discoveries was shared with the Protestant Reformation when widespread political and social upheavals further disturbed European culture. The dramatic impact of the Copernican revolution on the general public was caught in John Donne's lines from *Anatomy of the World,* published in 1611 CE – also the year in which the King James authorized version of the Bible was published to eliminate the confusion of alternate versions that were then in use. The poet's own confusion reads:

> *And new philosophy calls all in doubt;*
> *The element of fire is quite put out;*
> *The sun is lost, and th' earth, and no man's wit*
> *Can well direct him where to look for it.*
> *And freely men confess that this world's spent.*
> *'Tis all in pieces, all coherence gone,*
> *All just supply, and all relation.*[1]

The rising tide of scientific and technical discoveries that accompanied the Enlightenment prompted the disturbing problem of reconciling the new vision with the Scriptures and with common-sense attitudes. The earliest attempt at coping with eventful change was the suggestion that the unfolding picture of the natural world was already established in the original creation. The term for this conclusion was Deism. At first it was characterized as a clockwork solution, patterned after the mechanical clock with its programmed registering of time unaffected by the changes of the seasons in the natural order. Philosophically, the attempt at accommodation was addressed in Descartes' occasionalist theory in which the Creator was viewed as arbitrarily coordinating current temporal events in line with traditional time

---

1. John Donne, *Anatomy of the World*, 1611.

lines by means of divine intervention. The Deist move could also be traced in John Newman's monumental researches and linear measurements conveyed in his *Principia* of 1687. His scientific reputation rested principally through his discovery of the law of change in motion, the law of gravity, which was found to be applicable throughout the entire universe.

Some creationists as late as the twenty-first century still attempt to discredit the theory of evolution by asserting that God is the creator of every detailed event in a young Earth in every moment of time. In making this appeal for an all-encompassing divine order of creation these scholars are in effect presenting a picture of nature and history that anomalously resembles the naturalist view that all events are governed by determinist natural law. Their point of view is often accompanied by a confident attitude that assumes every problem or irregularity experienced in the flow of events can be removed by a technical fix. The Deist attempt to maintain an original harmony between Bible and emergent events fails to impress in this age of digital measurement and instant worldwide communications whereby we harmonize our relation to the procession of events.

EINSTEIN AND AFTER

A parody on the name of Einstein may be deemed excusable in light of his prominence and the relatively startling move he made in cosmological thinking. This eventuated in the transformational perceiving of "one stone becoming indeterminate quanta."

Einstein's papers on special and general relativity, 1905 and 1915, raised disturbing views when he probed the two most basic sensibilities of humans – space and time. In simplest explanation, it was his contention that only the first instance of an entity could be regarded as a standard. The second instance, though technically identical, could only be described relative to the first. The first instance need not, and should not be justified relative to the second. In the case of number series, number one is the numerical standard to which successive numbers are relative. Confusing as this may have appeared, it was more than matched in 1927 by a study developed by Werner Heisenberg who elaborated a general principle of uncertainty. From a quantum perspective he examined subatomic particles, discovering that two identical ones fail to share identical measures as to position and momentum. The variance suggested that individual particles (quanta), possessing an identical specificity, may in a given process be affected by the tools and attitudes of an agent to yield a distorted or different effect.

This conclusion raised serious doubts about the reliability of judgments employed in our highly technological societies. The lack of precision at the most elemental level of matter raised questions about the confidence of scientists in their methodologies.

The finding even called in question absolute unwavering relationships such as cause and effect, and subject and object, so basic to the conduct of empirical science, especially the science of engineering. David Hume could now be given credit for his doubts about apparent transfers from cause to effect that he had assigned to habits of mind. The assumption that a magisterial subject can lay claim to an object and manipulate it at will also came into question. It would appear that understanding the causal transaction may sometimes require interest and desire, time, and education comparable somewhat to the socializing involved in the case of alien personas achieving linkage and compatibility.

It is a matter of record that Einstein himself could not rest with the ambiguities of quantum theory to which his research had contributed. To the end of his career he continued the search for an encompassing equation that could be applied to remove any remaining uncertainty about natural events and experiences. On the morning of his death at age seventy-six (on 18 April 1955), his dead hand was found to be clutching a sheaf of notes bearing trial equations which he had mulled over before his last sleep.[2]

At the same time as the microcosm was being explored to an infinite degree, more expansive views were calling for extension of spatial perspectives far in advance of those raised in the great age of geographic exploration, or even later in space travel. Increasingly

---

2. Walter Isaacson, *Einstein: His Life and Work* (New York: Simon and Schuster, 2007), 431.

scientists have probed the vastness of space and time. For many years extending even to the recent past, some astronomers held a steady-state theory covering the phenomena of the universe. Some people holding secular and atheistic views favoured this earlier assumption that there is neither a cosmic beginning nor ending because that view eliminated conjecture about a transcendent agency. A dramatic shift came in 1965 when Arno Penzias and Robert Wilson, studying background microwaves discovered in space, concluded that the universe had emerged from a vast fireball exploding over 13 billion years ago. This judgment is now referenced with broad scientific agreement, although only belated acknowledgement has credited Georges Lemaître, Jesuit priest and physicist, with his 1930s predictive claim that the universe is expanding.

Since 1965 further studies of the cosmic microwave background have charted planetary development within the solar system and the birth of galaxies that continue to unfold. With the aid of Hubble and successive space probes a spatio-temporal map of cosmic development has unfolded in remarkably precise terms. From studies enhanced by the Planck spacecraft of 2009, latest estimates have dated the originating Big Bang with remarkable precision at 13.706 billion years ago. With assignment of the colour black to vaguely perceived spatio-temporal masses, the stuff and intelligibility assigned to the human sphere is limited to 4.9% of the universe, dark matter to 26.8%, and dark energy, accounting for the indeterminate remaining mass, at 68.3%.[3]

Turning to the more immediate interest we have in the development of our planet and emergence of human life forms, it is an arresting disclosure to view a temporal outline depicting how world phenomena and human development have unfolded over major time sequences. Arthur Peacocke, Cambridge chemist and devout Anglican priest, used the model of a forty-eight-hour clock to date life stages on planet Earth:

The model begins at Day One with algae appearing 600 million years ago. The carboniferous period begins 300 million years ago at the beginning of Day Two; at 8 PM of Day Two fish appear in the waters; at one minute to midnight of Day Two a primate stands upright; and, in the final thirty seconds, *Homo sapiens* appears and starts to use tools as the midnight bell begins to toll.[4]

A further note on the expansive reach of our human perspectives is reflected in the knowledge that our genetic heritage goes back to ancient forebears of our species, and our human DNA imprint links us with multiple living species originating on land, sea and air.

In the face of such awesome visioning the religious response might for many people be summed up in an overwhelming shrug suggested by the Hindu vocaliz-

---

3. Ken Tapping, "Mapping the Big Bang," *Skygazing: Astronomy through the seasons* (National Research Council of Canada: Penticton, 20 April 2013).
4. A.R. Peacocke, *Science and the Christian Experiment* (London: Oxford University Press, 1971), 72.

ation, *neti neti,* or perhaps in the articulate development of a negative theology. In fact, saying what God is not and what God does not do can appear more devout than confident expositions of a practiced creed, including eschatological scenarios, responding to questions that have not been asked.

In Christian theology the search for the right words need not be surrendered in silence, but we do need to be cautious in claims made for a theodicy based on *evidences.* There is a distinct lack of piety in the way many events are upheld as exemplars of divine foreordination. Many happenings are credited to divine providence based on a belief that every event, big or small, fits within a divine master plan. In effect, this perspective may often have the outcome of blaming God for monstrous disasters and suffering. At other times, favourable occurrences have been ascribed to God's almighty power, unmindful of the biblical terms that portray a weak God rather than a conqueror. The Hebrew exiles returning from Babylonian captivity were assured that "a little child shall lead them" (Isaiah 11:6). In similar vein, Jesus' preaching on the mount proclaimed assured blessedness that would fall to the mourner, the meek, and the persecuted (Matthew 5:3–12).

The ecological philosopher and Passionist priest, Thomas Berry, took a position in which he fully accepted the naturalist description of the universe in terms of the new cosmology. Based on this assumption he suggested that a modest view of benign ordering, or *providence* should be ascribed to the evolving universe itself. He claimed that the basic mood of the future might well be one of confidence in a continuing natural revelation that takes place in and through the earth. He wrote:

> If the dynamics of the Universe from the beginning shaped the course of the heavens, lighted the sun, and formed the Earth, if this same dynamics brought forth the continents and seas and atmosphere, if it awakened life in the primordial cell and then brought us into being and guided us through the turbulent centuries, there is reason to believe that this same guiding process is precisely what has awakened in us our present understanding of ourselves and of this stupendous process.[5]

(A retreat I spent with Berry and friends was memorable for hearing similar expressions.) Berry's emotional sense of belonging to the Earth has a counterpart in James E. Lovelock's appeal to regard the planet as a living entity. In his use of the Greek root term for the Earth, Gaia, Lovelock calls for a deep concern for the health and durability of the Earth.[6] He concludes that although an abused Earth may be able to regain

---

5. *The Dream of the Earth* (San Francisco: Sierra Club Books, 1988), 137.
6. J.E. Lovelock, *Gaia: A New Look at Life on Earth* (Oxford: Oxford University Press, 1979).

homeostasis like an animal recovering from injury or illness, the danger exists that one day the planet may well throw off its toxic predators. This, in fact, has already been happening to an alarming degree as we witness the increasing prevalence of both plagues and desertification.

The new cosmology of the twentieth century has received significant philosophical interpretation and support in the thought of Alfred North Whitehead, which received scholarly exposition by A.H. Johnson, who was my first teacher and mentor in philosophy.[7] Modern science, linked to technology and the life sciences, had already gone far in promulgating a culture of change when Whitehead elaborated his process philosophy. His approach drew upon a certain metaphysical optimism that had been out of fashion since the Enlightenment. Without providing a detailed exposition of Whitehead's thought, it can be characterized as strongly affirmative of natural history viewed in its forward drive to fulfill an organicist concept of the universe in its entirety. Taking support from the behaviour of subatomic particles, he made the claim that each event in the universe has an effect on every other event in the universe. The expenditure of energy that carries the world forward is held to be a tax upon all temporal subjects, while yet pressing forward to attain the benign goal of increasing truth, beauty and goodness. The process account embraces

---

7. A.H. Johnson, *Whitehead's Theory of Reality* (Boston: Beacon Press, 1952).

the antecedent perceptive nature of God together with the consequent unfolding of eventualities that may be recognized as completion of the divine nature.

As a Platonist, Whitehead expressed sentiments that sounded congenial with his earlier Christian formation. He confessed "there can be no doubt that the power of Christianity lies in its revelation as fact that which Plato divined in theory."[8] Whitehead affirmed the immanence of God and of God's involvement in the world as a participant and sufferer enduring all the strains of historical process. In effect, he gave an affirmative answer to the ancient question asked by some of the Church Fathers concerning whether God is impassive. The process view is that God has been present in successive levels of natural development. Since evolutionary steps, once established, cannot be reversed, history and nature as a whole are forever engaged in a forward process.

Prominent among theologians who appropriated the process model was Charles Hartshorne. He held a view of historicity in which God is viewed as carrying the history of human beings forward in God's memory of them. This constituted his version of eternal life for the individual. During an interview with Hartshorne in his ninetieth year (at his residence in Austin, Texas, April 1987), he responded to my question concerning his view of deconstruction, then current in literary and theological discourse. He strongly deplored the

---

8. A.N. Whitehead, *Adventure of Ideas* (Harmondsworth, Middlesex: Penguin Books, 1942), 196–197.

fact that deconstructionists lack a sense of history. He affirmed the authoritative role of memory in the developing processes of nature as a whole.

A postmodern voice claiming to bypass traditional distinctions between subjective and objective perceptions of reality has been that of the quantum physicist, David Bohm.[9] He discerned a twofold division within reality as a whole, assigning to it the terms *explicate order* and *implicate order*. The explicate order is the level at which we use descriptive analytical methods to explore phenomena. The implicate order is the vast teeming underlayer of reality of which we are only marginally aware, but which informs, inspires and energizes our engagement within the explicate order. It is from the implicate order that major discoveries or revolutions have their origin. In his view it is the source from which spiritual discovery and expression arises. The language of such experience is expressed pre-eminently in relational, exploratory and emotive terms.

Further evidence of the implicate order is discerned when we consider how our knowledge of our world environment has had to wait upon personal maturation and discovery. The process of gaining an education has increasingly involved advance through participation and practice. The social sciences have been foremost in practice, notably psychology and psychotherapy. Theologically speaking, the desire to

---

9. David Bohm, *Wholeness and the Implicate Order* (London: Routledge, 1980).

communicate in spirit and truth leads us to attend to the implicate order and to the potential of the Bible and its narration of stories witnessing to the faith of Israel and the Church. There we meet constant references to outstanding visions and experiences that await completion and meaningful disclosure: "There is still a vision for the appointed time; it speaks of the end and does not lie. If it seems to tarry, wait for it." (Habakkuk 2:3); "Now I know only in part; then I will know fully" (1 Corinthians 13:12).

This is in marked contrast with the classical Greek search for the ideal *telos* of history and the ultimate good. The Hebrew scriptures are an extended story of attempts by the chosen people to realize their destiny under tutelage of Sinitic laws and prophetic counsel. The script remains open awaiting messianic fulfillment. In the gospel, Jesus presents rabbinic teaching in the language of earthly-grounded parables. His message likewise remains open under the eschatological promise that the Holy Spirit will guide believers into all truth (John 16:13).

A significant advance in my own understanding of the theology of the past two centuries began early in my theological studies following an introduction to Kierkegaard studies. This occurred before my major commitment to research and teaching of theology. Ironically, Kierkegaard was discredited or ignored by most of his philosophical and theological peers considered in this review. On my part, I caught sympathetically the tone of Kierkegaard's mantra that "truth is subjectivity; subjectivity is truth," and his insistence that we know God only as subjects – and know Him only as the wholly other Subject. I read his views critical of the objectivity of Christendom, as represented in the national Church of Denmark. It was clear that he was critical of or indifferent to the claims of empirical science. That reserve in relation to science and the conviction that we know God only in the relation of immediate address became thematic in the existentialist philosophy and theology inspired by him. It can be traced through Buber, Barth, and Heidegger and their continuing influence through to the present.

A century after Kierkegaard, postmodern physics cast doubt on unqualified acceptance of objectivity at the heart of matter. It has been significant for me that my teacher, T. F. Torrance at Edinburgh, moved from his long sympathetic interpretation of Barth to add to his portfolio what he termed *theological science.* After accusing traditional theology for projecting a dualistic separation of an impassive God separate from the material world, he paid tribute to the new physics for releasing us from the dominance of empiricism. He claimed that today "Christian theology finds itself in the throes of a new scientific culture which is not antithetic to it, but operates with a non-dualistic outlook upon the universe, which is not inconsistent with the Christian faith, even at the critical points of creation and incarnation."[10] The view expressed here implies

---

10. T. F. Torrance, *Theology in Reconciliation* (Grand Rapids: Eerdmans, 1976), 270.

that the great spiritual events come as a surprise or astounding wonder; they are not repeated as a matter of course within natural law, but are revelatory.

Support for this view had scientific backing from another of my teachers, T. A. Goudge, a philosopher of biological science. He made the point that "narrative explanation enters into evolutionary theory at points where singular events of major importance for the history of life are being discussed .... The event is not an instance of a kind but is a singular occurrence."[11]

Methodologies of science have been fruitful in uncovering patterns of regularity in nature that empower human experiment and enterprise, but their recognition of uniqueness in natural happenings and human experience has been far less impressive. Ethical theories and moral actions tend to fall outside scientific categories and accompanying rigour. Pastoral empathy and clinical imagination are more clearly called for in coping with the issues at stake in threats to human survival and the health of the environment. Most ominous have been human failures to deal with threats to world peace posed by nations heavily invested in the science and instruments of war. This should be a special concern of Abrahamic peoples: those allied to the Prophet reverenced as the Compassionate and Merciful, those allied to the Shepherd King, and likewise the heirs of the Rabbi who proclaimed the sources of beatitude.

---

11. T. A. Goudge, *The Ascent of Life* (Toronto: University of Toronto Press, 1961), 71; 77.

After Words

THE FOREGOING REVIEW OF AN EPOCH-al period in modern theological engagement has served as a test of memory, but more importantly as a trial of judgments made in the course of a journey of faith. Reporting on the journey has been offered in part as recognition of teachers and students who have been companions on the way. I have been privileged to encounter and be sustained by communities of faith spread over venues and traditions in no fewer than six diverse countries.

In pursuing the foregoing study I have maintained my conviction that the historical approach is critical to any field of thoughtful inquiry. I have found the concept of history held by Gadamer and Ricœur to be convincing. Acquiring effective historical consciousness is a cumulative process. Sometimes it may involve forming a plot and story to illustrate and amplify meaning. Historical consciousness is gained by stages through reporting and making provisional analyses. The narrative continues.

Out of my historical experience of church and academy I feel bound to urge that theological study be pursued in historical dimension and in full view of the great issues that have been in contention. Without question, emphasis on spirituality and theological praxis current in preparation of candidates for professional ministry should retain importance, but I perceive a need to revisit the stern debates and vigorous contention that accompanied the diverging strands of theological emphasis during the twentieth century.

Theologically crafted debate was then especially intense regarding issues that ran heavily to political and ethical dimensions. These related to such terms as the Barmen Confession; apartheid; liberation theology; the advent of women to ordained ministry in Protestant churches; and questions regarding gender equality and identity.

Profound issues remain to be addressed with vigorous theological venting in forthcoming times. Prominent in human terms is the future of race relations encumbered with religious strife. Critical will be the ethical response to environmental dangers and the *universe* dimension of perils to planetary health. The uses and abuses of technological agencies in directing human enterprise and systems of organization will mount a major challenge for spiritual response.

During the past two centuries theology developed amid the tragedy of world war and the dissolution of cultural traditions which had been strongly anchored in religion. These events greatly speeded the secularity that had been advancing since 1500, the date assigned by Charles Taylor as the end to unquestioned religious belief among people in the Christian West. Moving into postmodernism, we have confronted general recognition of the end of Christendom as it was shaped in the Constantinian era.

On the positive side, however, by the beginning of the twenty-first century we can observe a major advance in religious belief and practice on a global basis. This applies especially to lands with exploding population growth in the eastern and southern global regions. Religious culture has been advancing along with postcolonial development, which has featured a great emphasis on education together with reassertion of traditional cultures. The Christian presence has followed the general pattern, at least in terms of population growth. The growth in ecumenicity has been greatly advanced by the new ease of world travel and the advance in educational standards and literacy.

A promising development in ecumenical commitment has been the addressing of socio-ethical issues on a global basis. The World Council of Churches began intensive research on these issues after World War II, eventuating in a global conference addressing *Faith, Science and the Future.* Three hundred participants, divided equally between theologians and scientists, were hosted in 1979 by the Massachusetts Institute of Technology. As a participant, I was blessed to experience the wisdom and energy devoted to this cooperative enquiry, which issued in a classic report.[1]

---

1. *Faith and Science in an Unjust World* (Geneva: World Council of Churches, 1980).

The global challenge to discern and express terms of the Christian ethic remains central to the Christian mission.

At the close of an extended review of the logos concerning *theos*, however, the critic may still find the key question to remain outstanding: Who is God and how does God relate to us?

For theology the issue will ever be the issue of how we attest to the being of God and how that relation governs our lives. For believing Christians the casual discard of the prime term *theos* has to be unsettling. We have become accustomed to hearing the dismissal of some theory or intellectual concept on the grounds of being mere theology. More disconcerting has been the decline in religious commitment registered in the rising statistic of persons identifying as atheists. A growing number of writers, some with scientific credentials, offer themselves as public intellectuals committed to the mission of saving their contemporaries from religious superstitions and the ignorance these represent.

They critique traditional theistic belief, which too often has pictured God in distant static objectivity. They evoke ridicule from light incursions into scriptural texts, especially highlighting the manner in which they are embraced by fundamentalists unacquainted with scientific interpretation. Moral failures observed in personal and statist dimensions are attributed to the establishment of religion – and especially to religions in conflict.

Recognizing and challenging this genre of literature, Scottish-born theologian John Macquarrie, writing in his Gifford Lectures,[2] criticized atheists for holding shallow, one-sided views of theistic belief. He found this to be a lingering of classical theology that rendered abstract views of God, remote in time and space, a blending of Hebrew monotheism and Greek conceptuality. The abstractness of the view represented an objectification lying open to empirical dismissal.[3]

Macquarrie maintained that God exists in dialectical relation with the universe and, likewise, in relation with the human subject. With broad recognition of the validity of religious experience he affirms that it offers varied attestations of the experience of God, such as both one and many, as present and absent, or as transcendent and immanent. In heeding this dialectic one can make discovery of meaning through the dialectical process comparable to the emergence of understanding gained through dialogue and discussion in juridical and diplomatic enquiry. Scientific debates proceed similarly from problem to solution.

Revealing a certain respect for mystical modes of thought, Macquarrie found that mysticism offers a striking picture of twofoldness in the perception of God. The blessed moment of religious ecstasy when God is perceived as overwhelmingly present may

---

2. John Macquarrie, *In Search of Deity: An Essay in Dialectical Theism* (New York: Crossroads, 1985).
3. James Farris, review of *In Search of Deity, an Essay in Dialectical Theism,* by John Macquarrie. *America* 153, Nov. 2, 1985.

be followed by the dark night of the soul when God seems to have deserted the beloved. The mystic may not herself feel disturbed by the temporal shifts in the path of realizing the fullness of her personhood. More importantly the believing community may value the mystic's rounded testimony and historical witness to the twofoldness of God, experienced as both transcendent and immanent.

Immanence may be the most compelling attribute of God for the devotee who indulges in nature worship and perceives every common bush alive with God. An extreme form of immanence may, however, pass into pantheism, which like some forms of idealism may fail to uphold the distinctness that characterizes values and judgements. Macquarrie guards against extending the concept of immanence to the point of removing difference and otherness in the relation of human beings and world. The point reflects the observation of the 19th century English divine, James Martineau, that pantheism is nothing other than a *solemn atheism*.[4]

The dialectical concept represents God as being relational at the centre of the divine nature, a relationship that is ever in process. The twofoldness of the relationship supports a distinctive manner of worship which can be at home with the Pauline evocation of the "goodness and severity of God" (Romans 11:22), or discernment of the *judging saving Word* (Bryden). The recognition of dialectic in the being of God ac-

---

4. James Martineau, *The Seat of Authority in Religion* (London: Longmans Green, 1890), 311.

cords with Trinitarian confessionalism and images of the Social Trinity. It removes the persistent tendency to perceive God with an immobile objectivity. It anticipates the *new thing* that we may yet experience in relation with God. We are a waiting people engaged in conversation with God.

Fraternal conversation can also be uplifting.[5] Macquarrie elaborates the concept of dialectical theism by showing how the dialectical relation is illustrated in our conversation with friends and colleagues. The engagement with God in prayer, whether privately or liturgically in community, is of this order. Bringing Christian principles to bear on ethical discourse and moral practice is always dialogical; and in interfaith engagement, dialogue has to be the way forward, free of advance reserve positions. We should likewise be restrained in the face of any appeal to write an authoritative systematic theology that embraces a dialectical modality. Reticence is called for in ecumenical and interfaith dialogue, especially if we heed the claim that silence may be a form of speech (Heidegger).

An earlier commitment to dialogical discourse could well have speeded the transition from the age that affirmed the right to invest in ownership of per-

---

5. During 1987, John Macquarrie and I enjoyed some intense conversations while sharing several weeks in the theological community of Austin, Texas. We realized that he and I had both completed doctoral studies in 1954, at the Universities of Glasgow and Edinburgh, respectively, prior to his impressive publications that had long been an important resource in my research and teaching.

sons, and from ages when constraint of gender rights deprived half the human population. Knowing God relationally involves commitment to a personal creed, which must be renewed continually in situations where we make moral decisions and assume spiritual responsibility within the believing community.

A theological review such as we have pursued must also remain mindful of the cultural hubris and triumphalism that too long lingered in theological expressions of earlier eras. Faithful pursuit of our theological quest calls for a humble spirit, avoiding any cadence of the Hebraic appeal to the Lord God of Armies. In speaking with God, whose name is Love, the conversant should speak in humble voice. The faithful pursuit of our theological task calls for the engagement to be pursued in the spirit and fellowship of prayer.

Having resorted earlier to Saint Augustine's directive on the nature of time, it is fitting at the end that we join him in devotional prayer:

> *O God, light of the minds that see you,*
> *Life of the souls that love you,*
> *And strength of the souls that seek you;*
> *Enlarge our minds and raise the vision of our hearts*
> *That with swift wings of thought*
> *Our spirits may reach you,*
> *The Eternal Wisdom.*

APPENDIX

A Path for Religious Dialogue

ON THE CONTINENT OF EUROPE AND in North America the thought of Martin Heidegger has excited interest far beyond the circle of professional philosophers. In the fields of linguistics, language, arts, history and religion his impact has been significant.

Extending the phenomenological method of Husserl, Heidegger discerns the fundamental mode of human existence to be bound up with the uncovering and articulating of the meaning of Being. Man, in his temporal and historical existence, represents the self-consciousness of Being, rendering Being, not as an abstraction or inferred substratum, but as concrete Being-in-the-world. He is sharply critical of the scholastic tradition in Western thought which has handed down the classical corpus in terms of exhaustive categories of judgment and in the language of assertion.

Originally published as W. J. S. Farris, "Heidegger on Language: a Path for Religious Dialogue," in *Malalasekera Commemoration Volume*, ed. O.H. de A. Wijesekera (Malalasekera Commemoration Volume Editorial Committee: Colombo, 1976).

By contrast, he sets himself the enterprise of probing the primordial, even mystical, foundations of human thought and its expression in language. His endeavour is to unfold a hermeneutic of *existence* in place of the logic of abstract conceptualism.

Heidegger finds the methodology and assumptions of empirical science to be largely hostile to his objectives. He criticizes the popular assumption that science occupies itself with real things. Instead he considers that science renders *things* abstract and virtually annihilates the *thing* itself, never allowing it to get *a hearing*. As he sees it, "Science always encounters only what *its* kind of representation has admitted beforehand as an object of science."[1] The task of a phenomenological account of reality will therefore be to give things a hearing through resolute application of the uncovering discernment of the human subject.

If Heidegger's philosophy is construed as the fulfilment of such a task, then it is obvious that his view of language is focussed throughout the whole of his work, although it may only be in the later Heidegger that the focus becomes markedly explicit. Our scope here will permit us merely to characterize the Heideggerian approach to language and to offer a suggestion concerning the direction it may provide in furtherance of inter-religious dialogue.

Already it is a matter of record within Christian circles in the West that Heidegger's perspectives have

---

1. Martin Heidegger, *Poetry, Language, Thought,* trans. A. Hofstadter (New York: Harper and Row, 1971), 170.

been utilized as a vehicle for religious expression. The earliest appreciation of Heidegger in this regard is associated with the thought of R. Bultmann, who was a commanding, if controversial, figure in Christian theological discussions of the 1940s and '50s, especially on the continent of Europe. Bultmann explicitly acknowledged his philosophical debt to Heidegger, his one-time colleague at Marburg.[2] More recently, a group of young theologians, notably H. Ott, the successor to Karl Barth at Basel, have engaged in seminar discussion with Heidegger on the implication of his philosophical work for religious thought.[3] In the English-speaking world, J. Macquarrie of Oxford[4] and L. Gilkey of Chicago[5] represent an approach to theology that is strongly paced by the structure of Heidegger's thought. Less directly related to Heidegger but belonging to a similar genre is the influential thought of P. Tillich, and in the Roman Catholic sphere, the work of such figures as B. Lonergan and K. Rahner. The latter typify a marked shift away from scholastic modes of thought toward a deeper understanding and analysis of human culture and self-consciousness.

The implications of such a shift in religious thinking in the West are significant for Christian involve-

---

2. Rudolf Bultmann, *Essays Philosophical and Theological* (London: SCM Press, 1955).

3. John B. Cobb & James M. Robinson, eds., *The Later Heidegger and Theology* (New York: Harper & Row, 1963).

4. John Macquarrie, *Martin Heidegger,* Makers of Contemporary Theology (London: Lutterworth Press, 1968).

5. Langdon Gilkey, *Naming the Whirlwind: The Renewal of God-Language* (New York: Harper & Row, 1970).

ment in inter-religious dialogue. Some of the stereotypes that have long informed mutual attitudes may now have to be seen as caricatures of current positions. The bearing of Heideggerian modes of thought will be pertinent to dialogue with some religions more than to others. The relevance to Christian–Buddhist discussion would seem obvious. Earlier Western thought, often clothed in terms of a *substance* philosophy, found it exceedingly difficult to comprehend Buddhist rejection of metaphysical objects and the idea of the discrete individuum. With a weakening of the logic of prescriptive conceptualism there may be an ampler base for appreciating what is involved in the claim that "the Tathāgata has no theories."[6]

LANGUAGE AND BEING

It is inappropriate to speak of a Heideggerian anlysis of Being or concept of Being. This would suggest a privileged position for the knower, giving him a free relation over against Being as that which is subject to his disposition. It is Heidegger's intention rather to uplift Being, to let it stand forth and be presenced, to let it be seen as the Being that it is. The phenomenological approach as he pursues it

> neither designates the object of its researches, nor characterizes the subject matter

---

6. *The Collection of the Middle-Length Sayings (Majjhima-nikāya)*, Vol. 1, trans. I.B. Horner (London: Pali Text Society), 67.

thus comprised. The word (phenomenology) merely informs us of the *'how'* with which *what* is to be treated in this science gets exhibited and handled.[7]

This distinguished the method of phenomenology from the special sciences in which there is an arbitrary bracketing of a specific subject-matter and its criteria, e.g., botany, geography, etc. The phenomenological method will attempt to carry through a primordial interpretation of Being, or hermeneutic of existence as the manifestation of being.

Man, the interpreter, is represented by Heidegger as *spokesman for Being.* He is able to speak in so far as he engages resolutely in the uncovering of Being as he encounters it in beings which are in the world. The classical Greek term for truth, *aletheia,* stood precisely for such a freeing or uncovering of beings. It is the function of language, in naming beings, to bring them for the first time to word and appearance.[8] In its poetic form, language most clearly illustrates the founding, establishing function of speech. Poetic speech belongs to the closest neighbourhood of man's being. In imaginative phrase, he describes the primordial role of such speaking as *the naming of the gods.* The elemental reality is by speech rendered articulate and brought to consciousness.[9]

In similar vein, Heidegger pictures language as *the*

---

7. Martin Heidegger, *Being and Time,* trans. John Macquarrie and Edward Robinson (London: SCM Press, 1962), 59.
8. Heidegger, *Poetry, Language, Thought,* 73.
9. "What is spoken purely is the poem." Ibid., 194.

house of being. It is the place of man's *dwelling,* rather than a manipulative tool or faculty of man which exists alongside others. It is an *a priori* structure of human existence:

> The nature of language does not exhaust itself in signifying, nor is it merely something that has the character of sign or cipher. It is because language is the house of Being, that we reach what is by constantly going through this house.[10]

Consequently it is never possible to analyze language exhaustively into its elements, even although Heidegger is often sensitive to the concrete etymologies of particular words. Speaking, as such, is primordial experience. This leads him to the frequent reiteration of the apparent tautology *language itself is language* or *language speaks.* It is not the case that language is designed for the sake of getting us somewhere but simply to show us where we are already. He elaborates the position:

> We leave the speaking to language. We do not wish to ground language in something else that is not language itself, nor do we wish to explain other things by means of language.[11]

---

10. Ibid., 132.
11. Ibid., 191.

All our speaking therefore must exercise a proper reserve, not forcing language or using it as the medium for a pragmatic or aggressive purpose. "We never come to thoughts. They come to us."[12] We dwell with language, attending to it, and allowing it to shape us as our master.

In his earlier writing, Heidegger had pointed to the inevitability of entering upon a hermeneutical circle in our quest of understanding. He regarded all interpretation as implying a fore-having, fore-sight, and fore-conception – so that it never is presuppositionless.[13] It appears that the later Heidegger found his position to be not fully consistent with his insistence that understanding and speaking is a *temporal* process, rooted in temporally conditioned existential concern. The use of grammatical tenses and the logical perspectives of foresight and hindsight may not illumine what actually takes place upon the pathway toward understanding. Of his own intellectual pilgrimage he has written:

> I have left an earlier standpoint, not in order to exchange it with another one, but because even the former standpoint was merely a way-station along a way. The lasting element in thinking is the way. And ways of thinking hold within them that mysterious quality that we can walk them

---

12. Ibid., 6.
13. Heidegger, *Being and Time*, 191–2.

forward and backward, and that indeed only the way back will lead us forward.[14]

The going back for thinkers of the Western tradition, will not simply be effected by historical research into what the Greeks have thought, in order to gain a classical perspective. Rather it is essential to think more originally than the Greeks – to out-Greek the Greeks as it were – the result being what is no longer, or never again will be, Greek.[15]

LANGUAGE AS DISCOURSE

Heidegger perceives the nature of language to be discourse. Unless one is engaged in dialogical speaking in which there is both articulation and the reserved disposition of listening, one is inclined to concentrate upon language itself and to render it into an object. Engaging in discourse with others is a primordial experience equivalent to having a state of mind or understanding. When discoursing with another person it is not simply the case that information, even about states of mind, gets to be shared. Instead, our being-with the other person, our co-state of mind with him, comes to be shared in *explicit* fashion.

True understanding and genuine discourse both

---

14. Martin Heidegger, *On the Way to Language*, trans. P.D. Hertz (New York: Harper and Row, 1971), 12.
15. Ibid, 39.

come under threat if we allow ourselves to lapse into *idle talk* and make no serious effort to hearken to one another. Hearing is a constitutive element in discourse, and only where hearing as well as speaking is an existential possibility can a discourse situation arise. In fact,

> Keeping silent is another essential possibility of discourse, and it has the same existential foundation. In talking with one another, the person who keeps silent can 'make one understand' … and he can do so more authentically than the person who is never short of words.[16]

Keeping silent effectively, holding oneself in reserve before the mystery of Being and before one's fellow being, involves entrusting oneself to the *drift of the dialogue,* permitting it to lead where it may. It involves undergoing an experience with the language. The important thing is that the dialogue should be kept constantly coming and that the speakers should construe themselves as occupying the role of messengers of Being.

Heidegger has made the poetry of his compatriot, Hölderlin, a subject of particular study, finding there a resonance with his own manner of viewing language. He quotes approvingly from the latter's "Celebration of Peace":

---

16. Heidegger, *Being and Time,* 208.

> *Much, from the morning onwards,*
> *Since we have been a discourse and have heard from one another*
> *Has human kind learnt; but soon we shall be song.*[17]

The conclusion suggested is that the dialogue of understanding issues not simply in clarification of meanings or sharing of information but in advancement to a higher state of consciousness and discernment of Being.

In a published reconstruction of a conversation held with a Japanese disciple and translator of his works, Heidegger offers some advice about the conduct of an East–West dialogue. He cautions against the tendency among some Eastern scholars to chase greedily after the latest news of what is happening in European philosophy. The only genuine dialogue will be one which presses mutual understanding back into the source of all thought. In the ensuing course of the conversation, his friend, Professor Tezuka of the Imperial University, Tokyo, begins to catch the point, and finally illustrates from his own experience:

> While I was translating, I often felt as though I were wandering back and forth between two different language realities, such that at moments, a radiance shone on me which let me sense the wellspring of re-

---

17. Heidegger, *On the Way to Language*, 78.

ality from which these two fundamentally
different languages arise was the same.[18]

The insight is offered as one which issues from the dialogical process, and not one which could be achieved by considering scientific or philosophical judgments about language.

In order to raise problematic questions concerning language, we necessarily possess language already and so are already conducting an interior dialogue. The paradox of language comes to focus when we reach the point of perceiving that the *being of language* and the *language of Being* are virtually one and the same.[19] Such a perception never permits us to assume that we can lay claim to the being of language. Language, like Being, is ever with us, yet also just ahead of us. The conditions of spoken dialogue, involving the mode of silence and waiting, govern to the end our appropriation of language.

TOWARD RELIGIOUS DIALOGUE

In light of Heidegger's view of the pathway to understanding, there may seem to be an inappropriateness about suggesting that his philosophical method be exploited for any specific objective such as the dialogue between religions. Moreover, it is a common claim

---

18. Ibid., 24.
19. Ibid., 72.

of manifold religions that they attend to what is primordial and purvey truth which is the language of the ultimately real. In Christian context, the attempt by Bultmann to demythologize the Christian symbols in the interests of a gospel of existential realization has already met with strong resistance. Can it be supposed that dialogue undertaken in quest of primordial understanding will be able to overcome the mutual resistance of alien doctrines and the asymmetry of historical and cultural developments in divergent religious experience?

Heidegger's way would be to suggest that there are existential concerns which outflank explicit comparisons of the language of symbol and myth. His ultimate criteria of judgment are not by any means free of ambiguity, viz., his distinction between *authentic* and *inauthentic* modes of existence. There may be no end to dialogue over the adequate reading of the language of Being, or hearing of the revelatory Word. But engagement in mutual listening and speaking may serve the modest end of revealing that some misunderstandings have been due to over-concentration upon historic linguistic usage. And it may be discovered that cultural experience in the late twentieth century is undergoing a convergence that may too often be cloaked by the persistence of formal structures that have been outgrown.

In so far as Heidegger has been effective in altering the cast of much Christian thinking, one may point to certain features of Buddhist thought which seem amenable to Christian–Buddhist dialogue in particular. One thinks of Buddhist rejection of a prescriptive logic, and the disengagement of the dhamma affecting man from any metaphysical assumptions. One notes too a possible placement in Buddhist psychology for the primacy which Heidegger gives to pure, foundational linguistic experience. Reference is to the faculty of intellect which is related to non-sensuous objects and yields a non-sensuous consciousness, differing from the consciousness afforded by the five empirical senses. It has been maintained with regard to the higher consciousness as construed in the central Buddhist tradition that

> Consciousness ... appears in coordination ... with its objective elements. It is (properly speaking) doing nothing. Nevertheless, we say that consciousness does cognize its object.[20]

This may serve as commentary to the saying from *The Dhammapada* concerning the mutuality of understanding and discursive thought: "Without knowledge there is no meditation, without meditation there is no knowledge."[21] Only the Way itself and not its signposts can lead to understanding.

Heidegger's chief contribution toward lighting a

---

20. T. Stcherbatsky, *The Central Conception of Buddhism* (Delhi: Motilal Banarsidass, 1970), 57.
21. *The Dhammapada*, trans. I. Babbitt (New York: New Directions Paperback, 1965), 55.

path for religious dialogue has been to show that the fundamental mood of human enquiry is coordinate with the path of religious piety. To wait upon *the holy* is to wait upon the word of disclosure. And that word, in its essential dialogical formation, is an attending together and speaking together out of the ultimate concern of existence.

About the Author

JAMES FARRIS IS PROFESSOR EMERITUS AT Knox College, University of Toronto, where he taught History and Philosophy of Religion for twenty-five years. This vocation followed graduate studies in Canada, Scotland, Switzerland and the United States. At an earlier period, as an ordained minister of the Presbyterian Church in Canada he fulfilled a ten-year teaching mission in Guyana and Jamaica, an experience strongly shaped by ecumenical and interfaith engagements. Following his retirement from teaching Farris served in several interim pastoral ministries, which included a two-year return to Guyana.

James Farris lives with his wife Jean in Charlottetown, Prince Edward Island.

Theological Places (cover)
Knox College, Toronto
New College, Edinburgh
Basel-Tor, neben an Universtät Basel
*United Theological College of the West Indies, Kingston, Jamaica

Layout and Typesetting: Kevin Farris
Cover Photographs: ©iStockphoto.com and James Farris*
Author Photograph: Cheryl Farris-Manning
Cover Design: Peter Farris-Manning

www.ingramcontent.com/pod-product-compliance
Lightning Source LLC
Chambersburg PA
CBHW072043290426
44110CB00014B/1561